Engineering the Victory March

Engineering the Victory March

Bangladesh Liberation War 1971

Brigadier R.B. Singh

THE BROWSER
Publishers and Booksellers
www.thebrowser.org

Title: Engineering the Victory March:
Bangladesh Liberation War 1971

Author: Brigadier Raj Bakhsh Singh

ISBN – 978-93-92210-03-7

Edition – I

Published by:
J.G.S. Enterprises Pvt. Ltd.
(Imprint: The Browser)

Publisher's Address:
SCO 14-15, Sector 8-C, Chandigarh 160009

Website: www.thebrowser.org
Email: service@thebrowser.org

THE BROWSER
Publishers and Booksellers
www.thebrowser.org

Dedicated to:

All the brave hearts who were part of
the 235 Army Engineer Regiment
for the Bangladesh Liberation War, 1971

'Sada Aage Sab Se Aage'

Contents

Foreword

By the nature of its employment during any operation, an engineer regiment gets parcelled out in smaller denominations to various formations in close support. A Sapper is a soldier first and, in addition, trained as a tradesman and made conversant with technical aspects of engineering tasks such as mine-laying, mine-breaching, bridging, constructing and maintaining tracks in varied terrains for ensuring quick movements for tanks, guns and vehicles. While not thus engaged, he may be deployed to hold ground, along with the formation, who he is meant to close support.

In such an event, the regiment misses all opportunities to document its performances and actions during a given operation, which is not the case for an infantry, armoured, or artillery formation. Thus, the regiment remains an unsung hero through no fault of its own and misses out on the recognition of the services rendered as well as the various lessons learnt for posterity.

This book, *Engineering the Victory March,* by Brigadier R.B. Singh, is an invaluable contribution in filling the void and bringing on record (no matter how late) the contribution made by the Sappers and 235 Army Engineer Regiment, in particular, during the liberation of Bangladesh. He has done well to briefly trace the political background, the overall strategy (evolution and contours of the plan), the preparation for the battle at the theatre level, the personalities involved, the implementation stage and the reasons for the overall success.

Against this canvas, he has covered, in great detail, the performance of his regiment, i.e., 235 Army Engineer Regiment. In the author's narration, one comes across emotional traces of his involvement with the men and the officers of the unit. It makes the writing more readable for laypeople who are not initiated in the art of soldiering.

I had the privilege to belong to this regiment and command the same soon after the war. Therefore, I congratulate Brigadier R.B. Singh on his effort.

Major General G.K. Sen (Retd.)
Ex-Colonel Commandant
The Bengal Sappers

Preface

It was a stupendous engineering feat displayed by the Corps of Engineers that ensured that the Indian Army rapidly advanced toward its aim of liberating Bangladesh at the earliest.

Engineering the Victory March brings out the role played by all the engineer regiments deployed in the Eastern Command, with the detailed functioning of my regiment, the 235 Army Engineer Regiment.

This regiment played a dominant and decisive role in carrying out innumerable sapper and infantry tasks to the entire satisfaction of the formations that it supported. We were the first ones to step into East Pakistan on 22 November 1971 and the last ones to leave Bangladesh in April 1972, after restoring full communication. We made as many as 27 bridges, neutralising all mines and IEDs (improvised explosive devices) and making all ferry sites functional on the road between Hilli–Gaibanda and Dinajpur–Dhaka (a distance of approximately 400 km).

All along, I had the urge to write and record the valour, determination and diligence of the rank and file in this operation. The officers and men did their task spontaneously with total disregard for their safety.

In this effort, I have received immense help not only from my regiment but also from officers and men from other formations and the regiments with whom I have operated. I collected and collated from written materials of senior formations to create the overall mosaic of the entire operation. Some senior officers have given me valuable time and personal guidance.

My special thanks to my wife Perminder and all my family members who gave me immense support in this endeavour, and especially to my three granddaughters Amareen Raj Kaur, Priyl Raj Kaur and Zoya Raj Kaur, who came running to help me whenever I got stuck in handling the computer.

As a war veteran, I have desired to share the battle experience with the young and the middle-rank officers of today and tomorrow. It may help posterity handle similar situations in the future pragmatically.

Brigadier R.B. Singh

Background to the Conflict[1]

Waqt karta hai parwarish barsoon
Hadsa ek dum nahi hota
—Qabil Ajmeri

(Time breeds tragedy over the years
It does not occur abruptly; out of the blue)

Most storms gather rapidly, in a matter of hours, but some only after a day or two. The one which led to the war of 1971 had been brewing for many years. Pakistan was an artificial entity that came into being with the partition of India following the demands for a nation for Muslims from the Indian sub-continent. However, the events leading to the 1971 India-Pakistan war and the emergence of Bangladesh were to show that Islam was not a sufficient bonding adhesive for the two entities – West and East Pakistan – separated by the huge land mass of India. East and West Pakistan were split along cultural,

[1] Sourced from *War Despatches 1971* (edited by Brigadier B.S. Mehta, Occam, 2021).

geographical and linguistic lines. The people in East Pakistan, belonging to erstwhile East Bengal, were more akin to West Bengal, both culturally and linguistically, and quite different to people residing in West Pakistan.

The Bengali-speaking majority of East Pakistan turned violent when Urdu was made the sole national language of Pakistan, sparking massive protests. Students at Dhaka University revolted and went on strike on 11 March 1948. Public meetings and rallies were banned. In 1952, when Prime Minister Khwaja Nazimuddin declared, in Dhaka, 'Urdu will be the state language', students at the Dhaka University again revolted. The police and paramilitary forces resorted to the use of brutal force and killed six students. The deaths sparked widespread civil unrest, led by the Awami Muslim League. After years of conflict, Pakistan's Central Government relented and granted official status to the Bengali language in 1956.

The Six-Point Proposal

The tensions between the Bengali population of East Pakistan and the dominant Punjabi residents of West Pakistan had taken root right at the creation of Pakistan. However, they gathered momentum in 1966 when the military leadership of West Pakistan refused to accept the Six-Point Programme for the autonomy of East Pakistan, championed by the Bengali leaders, led by Awami League's Sheikh Mujibur Rehman.

The Bengalis in East Pakistan were tired of being treated as second-class citizens and largely economically exploited. For instance, all the jute and tea grown in East Pakistan earned most of the country's foreign exchange, but the money was used to develop Pakistan's western wing. The more populous East Pakistan was even denied protection from floods and cyclones, which brought periodic devastation to life and property of its residents. Besides their differences in language and cultural habits from West Pakistan, the Bengalis desperately wanted autonomy for themselves in the east wing of Pakistan (see Appendix 'A').

Discriminatory Policies against East Pakistan

It would seem that the West Pakistanis had done just about everything they could to stoke animosity in their eastern wing instead of trying to assuage feelings of alienation. The problem between Pakistan's western and eastern wings was deep-rooted – in physical separation, different languages, and a lack of trust. The popular joke in the subcontinent was that the two wings were separated by a thousand miles but united by only three things – Islam, English, and Pakistan International Airlines! The long-standing discriminatory and exploitative policies led to a sense of alienation. A feeling of victimisation permeated due to disparity in Bengali representation in the civil services, defence forces and managerial positions. To make matters worse, the West Pakistanis scorned the

Bengali 'Bingo' as weak and unfit for soldierly duties. Even the Hindi-speaking people from Bihar, who settled in Bangladesh, did not merge with the Bengalis but continued maintaining closer relationships with the West Pakistanis.

Agartala Conspiracy

Another trigger was the Agartala Conspiracy Case – a sedition case framed against Mujib and other leaders of the Awami League by the Government of Pakistan in 1968. It resulted in protests, an upsurge and hostility, which forced Ayub Khan to withdraw the sedition case. When Mujibur Rehman returned from West Pakistan to Dhaka, after a prolonged stay in jail, he was given a hero's welcome and, after that, anointed with the endearing salutation of Bangabandhu. However, the upsurge contributed to the increasing Bengali nationalism, political unrest and agitations.

Impact of Cyclone *Bhola*

In the 12 months leading up to the liberation and birth of Bangladesh, several other events took place that hastened the complete disaffection of the population in the East. On 11 November 1970, Cyclone *Bhola* lashed East Pakistan. As a result of this, death and devastation were widespread. As per some estimates, the lives of over two lakh people ended in a watery grave. Total neglect by the West Pakistani military junta became the final straw for the emotional break. The Awami League converted this widespread negative disposition into a mass movement. The clash had virtually become civilian vs. military, Bengali vs. West Pakistan, popular democracy vs. military dictatorship, and non-violent vs. violent. While the east wing was immersed in fighting death, disease, epidemic, and starvation, the western wing was toasting the emergence of Zulfiqar Ali Bhutto.

Elections and their Aftermath

General elections were held in Pakistan on 7 December 1970 to elect members of the National Assembly. It was the first general election in the 23 years since the creation of Pakistan. Voting took place in 300 constituencies, of which 162 were in East Pakistan and 138 in West Pakistan. The result was a victory for the Awami League, led by Sheikh Mujibur Rehman, which won an absolute majority of 160 seats, all in East Pakistan; the Pakistan People's Party (PPP) of Bhutto won only 81 seats, all in West Pakistan. The then leaders of Pakistan, again all from West Pakistan (and PPP), strongly opposed the idea of a government led by anyone from East Pakistan. Bhutto uttered the infamous phrase '*Idhar hum, udhar tum* (We rule here, you rule there)' thus verbally dividing Pakistan for the first time. The Assembly elected in 1970-71 was, therefore, never convened at all.

Postponement of the Inaugural Session of the National Assembly and Operation Searchlight

On 1 March 1971, an indefinite postponement of the inaugural session of the National Assembly, scheduled to be held on 3 March, further electrified the atmosphere. Having put the seal of authenticity on the triumph of the Awami League, led by Sheikh Mujibur Rehman, now to deny it power was like building a sand wall to control the floodwaters of the mighty Ganges – an exercise in futility. The events took a severe and dramatic turn when, to control the lawlessness, the Pakistan Army launched Operation Searchlight on 25 March 1971 against the people of East Pakistan under Lieutenant General Tikka Khan, Governor and General Officer Commanding East Pakistan. On the same day, Mujib was arrested. The Army was given a free hand for using maximum force, resulting in the genocide of Bengalis. All domestic and international communications were cut off, and all Bengali troops were disarmed.

This operation was an overt attempt to kill the intellectual elite and Bengali nationalism. It resulted in mass killing of those targeted. The genocide launched by the Army led to the rape of half a million women, while millions escaped the fury of the Army by seeking refuge in India. Tales of the Pakistani Army asking the Bengalis to lift their *lungi* to display circumcision or demanding recitation of Muslim prayers, marking the houses of Hindus with H or forcing them to wear a black cloth to identify themselves as Hindus became very common.

These systematic acts of violence and bloodshed were aimed at eliminating the core of future resistance. Imagine a Pakistani general asking his troops, 'How many Bengalis have you shot today?'

The continuing military operations by the Pakistan Army resulted in a large-scale exodus of refugees, numbering nearly ten million, fleeing to India. Over 30 million were also displaced internally. Bangladesh Government figures estimate that the Pakistani Army killed some three million people. The financial burden of this refugee relief effort was estimated by the World Bank (as quoted in the New York Times) to be about $700 million in an entire year. This burden was roughly half of India's defence budget in 1970!

The Indian Strategy

By April 1971, the Indian leadership was convinced that a war with Pakistan was inevitable. However, there were two opposing views about when to wage war. One thought was that the Indian Army should commence operations at the earliest and assist the Bangladeshis who had launched their war of liberation. This view was generally advocated by the then Defence Minister Jagjivan Ram, Finance Minister Y.B. Chavan, some other Congress party leaders and some officers of the Border Security Force. The second view was of the Indian Army, particularly of its Chief, General Sam Manekshaw, who believed that the operations should be launched more deliberately after due planning and creating logistics infrastructure. For this, the Indian Army required six to nine months for preparations for an assured victory. It is to the credit of General Manekshaw that he had the courage to convince Prime Minister Smt Indira Gandhi about the time frame required for the sure success of this operation (see Appendix 'B' for details of Manekshaw's account of his subsequent briefing of Smt Indira Gandhi). The factors considered were as under:

- The Indian Army was oriented toward operations against West Pakistan and China, and only contingency plans existed to deal with East Pakistan. Hence, time was needed for reorientation, reorganisation, training, and creation of new logistic bases.
- The Pakistan Army had, by now, built up about four infantry divisions in East Pakistan.
- The monsoon was about to break, which would make the progress of operations difficult in the riverine terrain of East Pakistan. In addition, it was prudent to wait till the passes on the northern borders, opposite China, had closed.
- India had to create an international environment for a war. Such an environment did not exist in India's favour. Since the war with Pakistan would be an all-out war, all three military services would be involved. This required proper planning and preparations. Lieutenant General J.F.R Jacob, in

his book, *Surrender at Dacca,* says that at the time of the Bangladesh War, no institution of the Indian Army taught or studied strategy. Our military institutions taught tactics at the unit, brigade and, to some extent, at the divisional level. Consequently, no realistic, overall estimate of war situations by the Army Headquarters was made. There was, in fact, no strategic or political definition of policy nor an appropriate higher command organisation to plan or direct the war. Political objectives were rarely spelt out clearly. As a result, planning at the Service Headquarters lacked depth.

- Given the international climate and the possibility of the United Nations Security Council imposing a ceasefire, any campaign, to be meaningful and effective, had to be swift and of short duration. There was also a threat from the Chinese in the north and USA coming to help Pakistan. It was, therefore, stressed that the primary objectives should be communication and that the command centres and the approaches to these should be along subsidiary tracks so as to bypass the main centres of resistance. It was said that once the objective had been secured, a road axis could be cleared later.

By the end of May 1971, a draft plan based on the following strategic outline was made:

- The final objective could be Dhaka, East Pakistan's geopolitical and geostrategic heart.
- Thrust lines were to be selected to isolate and bypass Pakistani forces to reach the final objective.
- Subsidiary objectives were to be selected with the aim of securing communication centres and the destruction of the enemy's command and control capabilities. Fortified centres of resistance were to be bypassed and to be dealt with later.
- Preliminary operations were aimed at drawing out the Pakistani forces to the border, leaving key areas in the interior lightly defended.
- In the preliminary operations, whenever we attacked Pakistanis in their prepared defences, they fought with courage and doggedness. The attack on Hilli defences, which commenced on 22 November, was finally cleared on 11 December with very high casualties. These preliminary operations reinforced Eastern Command's strategic concept that fortified positions had to be bypassed as they took a long time and great cost to reduce.
- Fortunately for us, the Pakistanis had concentrated their troops in the towns. Had they chosen to defend approaches to the river crossing sites, we would not have been able to cross the rivers and reach Dhaka.
- From 25 March onwards, a large number of refugees were crossing the border and there was no

semblance of an international boundary. East and West Bengal had emotionally united and the latter was keen to help their brethren across the border.

Everywhere there was a vast sea of humanity; half-dressed and oblivious to the surroundings. Their poverty was visible, their condition pitiable. Apparently, for them, freedom from British rule had been a hallucination, without any benefits. After seeing them, I was reminded of a poem:

Yeh galion ke awara bekar kutte
Keh bakhsha gaya jin ko zauq-e-gadai
Zamane ki phathkar sarmaya inka
Jahan bhar ki dhutkar inki kamai
Yeh muzlum mukhluk gar sar uthai
To insan sab sarkashi bhool jai
Yeh chaheen to dunya ko apna bana leen
Yeh aaqaon ki haddian tuc chaba leen
Koi inko ehsas-e-zillat dila de
Koi inki soi hui dum hila de.
—Faiz Ahmed Faiz

(Stray street dogs,
importune beggars by birth.
Contempt has been their lot
from the beginning of time
and wretchedness their only reward.
If only they would revolt

and teach the arrogant man a lesson –
tear his fancy clothes,
bury their fangs in his bones.
If only someone would make them
see their terrible degradation.)

The whole countryside was in revolt. It was viewed that, during the elections, a politically emotional approach based on 'Hate Punjabi shalla' carried the day.

Pakistani Army Major General Hakeem Arshad Quershi, in his book, *The Indo-Pak War 1971*, says:

> I can distinctly recall the lament of a sensitive Pakistani, a vendor of cheap spectacle frames, in reaction to the culture of loot that had taken over immediately after Partition. He had no hesitation in proclaiming, on every street corner, a dubious future for his newborn country. In his inimitable voice, he would recite the following soul-stirring verses:
>
> *'Chor, uchakay chaudhri*
> *Tai lundi run pardhan*
> *Luche bun gai uche*
> *Tai kanjar marasi bun gai khandaan.'*
>
> (Thieves and confidence tricksters
> are now the leaders,
> and prostitutes have become chieftains. Characterless
> individuals have
> become men of position,

and professional singers and dancers
are now the symbols of honour.)

> The Muslims of India created a country, a miracle, through the free expression of individual and collective will. At the time of the Partition, however, Maulana Abdul Kalam Azad, had forecast that the new country would disintegrate in 25 years. His prediction came uncannily true. How had he been able to prophesy our demise so precisely? Had he been encouraged by our lack of ability to govern, or was his opinion founded on the 'fallacy' of the genesis of Pakistan? Was he prompted by economic reasons, or was it an expression of his confidence in the conspiracy that the Congress had hatched the moment the inevitability of Pakistan was realised? The Maulana is no more with us to clarify his prophecy, but our rank incompetence as administrators and our selfishness as individuals did, over the years, definitely contribute to the initiation of insurgency in East Pakistan.

Incidentally, Major General Qureshi, during the 1971 war, was commanding 26 Frontier Force (FF), which was responsible for the defence of Hilli. In the second week of June 1971, the defence of Hilli was handed over to 4 FF, and 26 FF was moved to defend Dinajpur. Dinajpur didn't fall till 16 December and was made to surrender. For his act of bravery in the defence of Dinajpur, Qureshi was awarded the Sitara-i-Jurat, Pakistans's second-highest gallantry award equivalent to our Mahavir Chakra.

Preliminary Actions

General (SHFJ) Sam Manekshaw, the Indian Army Chief, having conferred with his two counterparts, the Naval Chief, Admiral S.M. Nanda and Air Chief Marshal, P.C. Lal, and after many deliberations, cautioned against haste since many factors were involved. By then, the subcontinent was in the summer of 1971, and the harvested grain needed to be moved across the country. The trains and road transport could either ferry the grain or the troops to the battle. Once the monsoons set in, the movement of India's military units would be hampered, especially in the riverine terrain of East Pakistan. Moreover, The Indian Armed Forces needed to upgrade their military inventories with new weapons and platforms to confront Pakistan's better-equipped armed forces that had received superior war fighting systems, mostly made in the US.

As the armed forces began to prepare for what indeed became a historic victory, Smt Gandhi took up the job of winning the world's support for India's humanitarian initiative in East Pakistan. It wasn't easy with the US supporting Pakistan, especially after Pakistan had helped President Nixon's National Security Adviser, Henry Kissinger, to open diplomatic dialogues with China in July 1971.

Recognising the importance of international backing for its military campaign, Smt Indira Gandhi and her Foreign Minister, Swaran Singh, visited many world capitals in 1971, including Washington DC. She was cold-shouldered by the Nixon-Kissinger combine because of America's strategic interests in Pakistan – a CENTO (Central Treaty Organisation) and SEATO (Southeast Asia Treat Organisation) ally. However, it was finally in August 1971 when her diplomatic efforts bore serious fruits – New Delhi signed the Indo-Soviet Treaty of Peace, Friendship and Cooperation with Moscow (see Appendix 'C'). Though the war officially started on 3 December 1971, following simultaneous Pakistani air raids on Indian air bases in the north and west of India, military operations along the borders of East Pakistan had started in the last week of November 1971.

On 25 March 1971, when Operation Searchlight was launched against the people of East Pakistan and Sheikh Mujibur Rehman was arrested, the civilian population protested en masse, along with the para militia, namely the East Bengal Regiment (EBR). India was burdened with millions of East Pakistan refugees and had to grant shelters to the refugees along with many armed contingents of the East Pakistan militia. Soon these armed contingents, along with civilian leaders, many of them elected as members of their National Assembly, and belonging to the Awami League, realised that without the Indian Government's help, it may not be possible to attain independence from Pakistan. So, the Indian Government extended them a helping hand.

These para militias, mostly ex-EBR, fighting for freedom in their way, were known as Muktiyoddhas

Fighters (MF). Besides these, other young civilians of East Pakistan joined the armed struggle to be known as freedom fighters. These newly inducted people were recruited chiefly by their civilian leaders, including their elected MNAs. To help them, the FF personnel were given basic arms/ammunition training centrally somewhere in India. After receiving such training, they were dispatched to various sectors/sub-sectors to carry out arms insurgency, sabotage and other such activities targeted against the Pakistan Army.

Mukti Bahini and Mukti Fauj are the same. The word *bahini,* in Bengali, means army or *fauj.* This combined group of people, comprising the MF/FF and those units of the Indian Army which took part in liberating (*mukti*) East Bengal from Pakistan, was the Mukti Bahini in the strict sense, though we mean only the MF/FF combined. There were officers and JCOs (junior commissioned officers) of EBR also in this group, and some FF was also given the status of officers. The senior-most officer was a colonel who was the commander-in-chief (C-in-C) of the MF and FF personnel group. Officers with the rank of a major were sector commanders from their side. Following months of training imparted to Bengali guerrillas of the Mukti Bahini and some other groups who had come into India with the refugees, now their military operations picked up considerable momentum by November 1971. The Battle of Garibpur on 21 November and the Battle of Hilli on 22 November occurred before the war was officially declared.

The Mukti Bahini played a stellar role in the Liberation War of Bangladesh. They provided crucial information about the terrain, deployment pattern, and enemy strength at various places and their activities. They also carried out various disruptive activities such as sabotage, blowing bridges and ferries, laying of nuisance mines and blowing off vital installations to deny their use by the Pakistani Army. In a nutshell, they helped to make life miserable for the Pakistani Army so that the latter could not operate and rest in peace.

For any campaign to succeed, certain parameters must be assessed before launching an operation. These include the **terrain** where our troops were to operate, the **strength and deployment** pattern of the enemy troops, their capability, and the equipment held by them, and finally, the **mood of the people** where we were to operate.

When I say mood, I mean whether they would be hostile or would support our actions. In our case, the mood of the Bangladeshi people was quite favourable to India, as our Army was going to help them in their war of liberation against the ruthless leaders of West Pakistan. Therefore, they welcomed our Army, enabling us to operate more freely and without any hostility from the locals. The Mukti Bahini and the locals acted as our eyes and ears and helped us on many occasions to make our campaign successful.

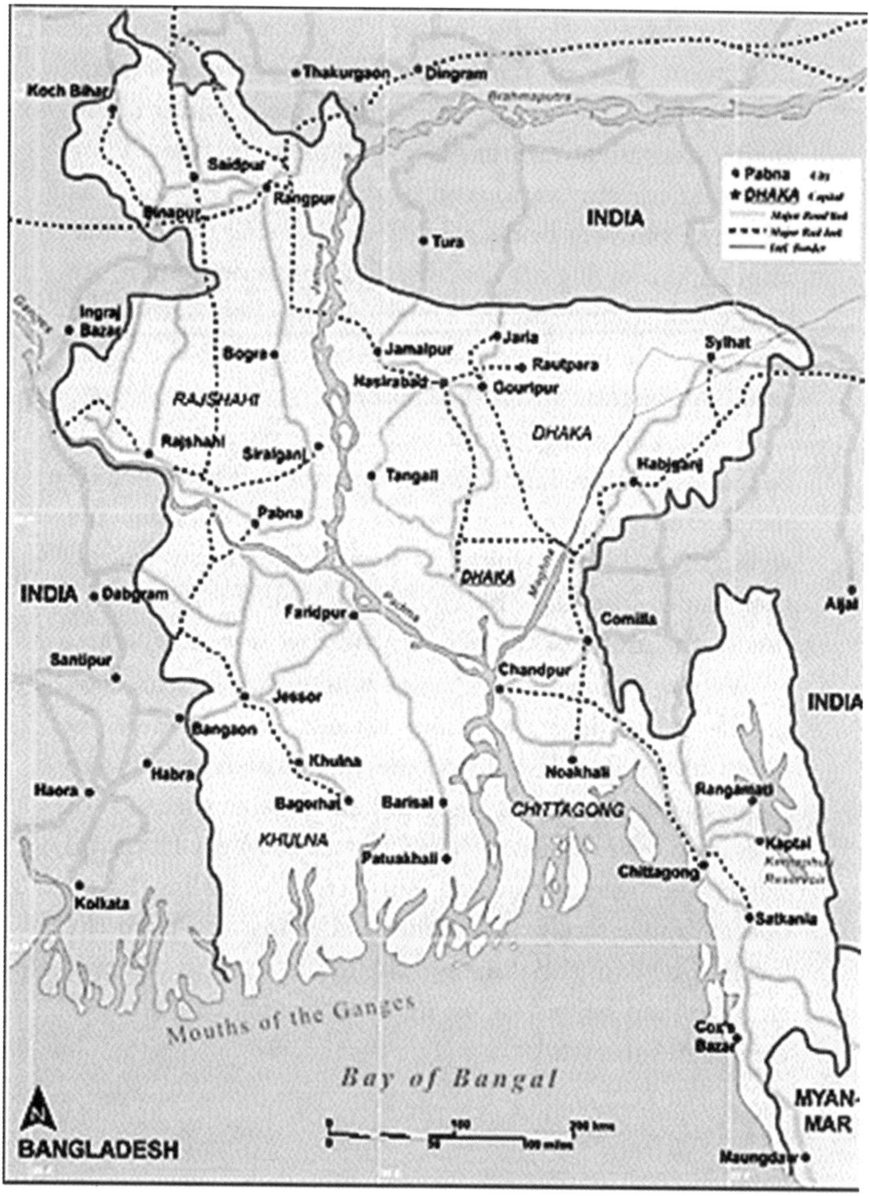

Koch Bihar
Thakurgaon
Dingram
Brahmaputra
Saidpur
Rangpur
Dinapur
Pabna
DHAKA
INDIA
Tura
Ingraj Bazar
Jamalpur
Jaria
Sylhat
Bogra
Rautpara
Nasirabad
Gouripur
RAJSHAHI
DHAKA
Rajshahi
Siraiganj
Tangail
Habiganj
Pabna
DHAKA
INDIA
Dabgram
Faridpur
Comilla
Aijal
Santipur
Chandpur
Jessor
INDIA
Bangaon
Khulna
Noakhali
Habra
Haora
Bagerhat
Barisal
CHITTAGONG
Rangamati
KHULNA
Kaptal
Patuakhali
Chittagong
Kolkata
Satkania
Mouths of the Ganges
Cox's Bazar
Bay of Bangal
MYAN-MAR
BANGLADESH
Maungdaw

Plan for the Liberation of Bangladesh

Erstwhile East Pakistan was not the easiest of campaigning grounds. That is why, during the initial stages, the brief given to the Eastern Command, by the Indian Army, was limited. The aim was to occupy only two areas of East Pakistan, that is, Chittagong and Khulna, the two entry ports, so that an interim government of Bangladesh could be established.

Terrain and Challenges

Initially, the capture of the whole of East Pakistan was not conceived as the major problem was the geography and terrain of East Pakistan. Three major rivers – the Padma (or Ganga), Jamuna (or the Brahmaputra), and the Meghna, along with their many distributaries and channels, carve East Pakistan into four natural riverine regions. The main rivers are so wide that, at places, the far bank cannot be seen. Each sub-region is further divided into several pockets, cut by smaller rivers and their distributaries. Communication across these natural obstacles is restricted to ferries and large river crafts plying through known navigable channels. There are no bridges across these rivers except for the Hardinge Rail Bridge

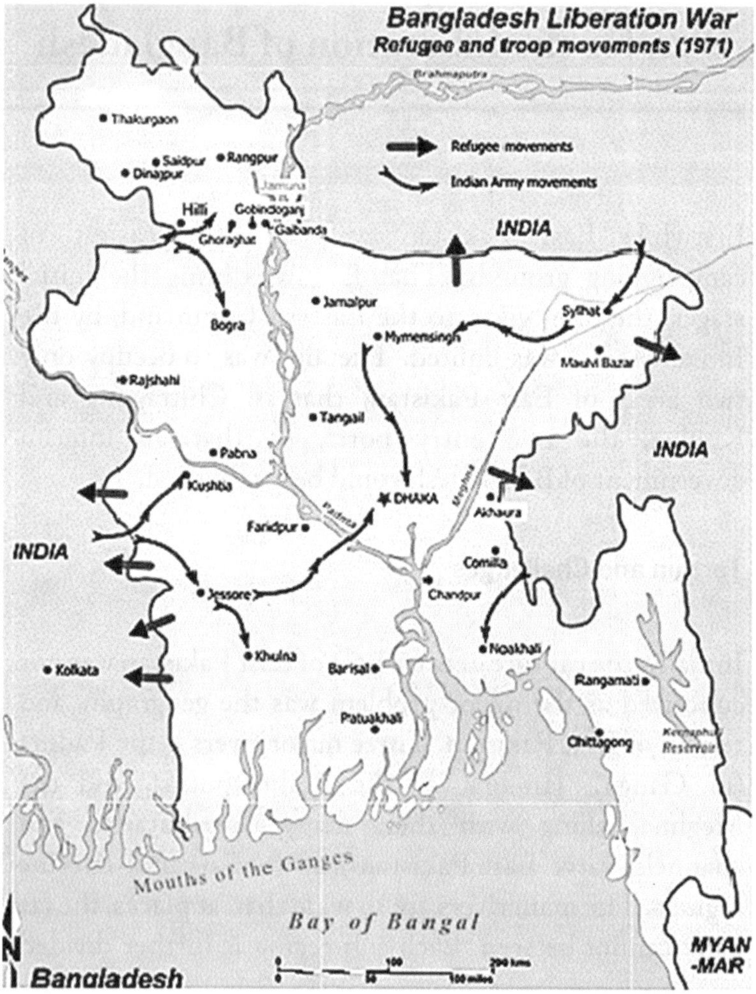

over the Padma River and the Ashuganj Rail Bridge over the Meghna River.

During those days, East Pakistan had a poor and ill-maintained road communication system, which was secondary to the water and rail transport system. In fact, for road and rail communication, not much attention was paid to East Pakistan after the Partition in 1947. The fury of the monsoons made the cost of maintaining these roads prohibitive. Good roads ran only a few miles out of the significant towns, after which their state deteriorated. Rural and municipal roads were rarely paved. There were only five all-weather roads, and that too, of a single lane. They crossed minor rivers and streams, again and again, which were as wide as 1,000 ft (300 m).

Bridges did not exist at most of the crossing places. The road transport had to be ferried across. Most roads were on embankments, as the area around was low-lying and became marshy and waterlogged during the rains. Movement off the road was challenging. By November 1971, many ferries and bridges were demolished, some by the Pakistani troops and a fair number by the Mukti Bahini in their attempts to disrupt communications in East Bengal. There were no direct road links between the four riverine sectors. However, all sectors were linked by inland water transport (IWT).

The region experiences heavy rainfall of over 250 cm annually, and almost 75 per cent of it occurs during monsoons (June–September). During October–November, the weather tends to be cyclonic, causing torrential downpours and giving rise to very high wind velocity. During dry weather, a limited cross-country movement, with prior reconnaissance, is feasible. Still, even a light shower can bring all cross-country moves to a halt because of a very high water-table. The terrain configuration imposed severe restrictions on any large-scale movement between the forces' sectors, separated as they were by the major rivers. Therefore, more or less independent operations were planned in the four sectors, later converging and culminating in a concerted thrust towards Dhaka.

The idea that an attacking army could bridge these rivers/streams, fight the enemy, and take territory within a couple of weeks was simply impossible. Aptly described as an 'Engineers War', such a rapid offensive in a riverine country with poor roads and antiquated bridges would have made no headway but for the traditional skills of the Sappers in improvisation.

Pakistani defensive positions covered the main routes of ingress. Conventional operations against such positions would have been time-consuming and expensive in terms of casualties. Therefore, the bold decision to bypass these positions and effectively penetrate the main road was taken. A strategy of 'Rushing Torrent' was adopted, which visualised bypassing major opposition and turning flanks of the enemy by deep penetration. The main issue in successful execution was the ability of the force to move cross-country and sustain itself. It became the crucial facet of all engineer appreciations and assessments.

The major concern of the Engineer Planning Staff, at the highest level, got focused on the availability of suitable bridging equipment, the capability of the road systems for cross-country movement of the various arms, and the availability of engineer troops. There were seven divisions, the 101 Communication Zone Area, and an independent brigade deployed in the Eastern Command, with 18 other engineer regiments, 411 Para Field Company, and a host of minor units like engineer plant companies, engineer workshop and park companies, engineer parks, bridge company normal, ASC battalion, transport company ASC (Tipper), bomb disposal platoons and IWT companies. It worked out to almost three times the usual allotment of engineer troops. The terrain configuration of East Pakistan was so challenging that moving cross-country against the grain of the country required adequate bridging, track material and sufficient engineer troops. Else the advancing formations would be held up, losing precious time. Adequate engineer troops were also required to breach mine fields, lay mine fields, remove nuisance mines, booby traps, and IEDs, maintain tracks and a host of other planned and unplanned tasks.

The bridging equipment available was Folding Boat Equipment (FBE) and Bailey Bridge of World War II vintage. However, the scenario changed with 130 mm medium guns, towed by Kraz and T-55 tanks. Only a limited quantity of the Krupmann heavier assault bridges was available, which was barely adequate for use in one sector. A conscious decision was, thus, taken to restrict the use of T-55 medium tanks only in the II and XXXIII Corps Zones.

Later, capturing the whole of East Pakistan became the ultimate aim of the offensive in the east. Towards this aim, multi-pronged thrusts were planned, i.e., XXXIII Corps from the northwest, II Corps from the southwest, 101 Communication Zone Area from the north, and IV Corps from the east.

The four thrusts were planned to mesh in with the four riverine sectors into which the Padma, Jamuna, and Meghna rivers divided the country. Each thrust was to be independent of the other, and each was to converge and culminate in a concentrated thrust towards the aim of the offensive – Dhaka, East Pakistan's capital and geopolitical heart. The cross-country going, in a riverine terrain, where even minor rivers often measured 1,000 ft wide, where there were numerous marshes and water-logged rice fields, presented a Herculean challenge. From the outset, improving and constructing tracks and bridges emerged as the most pressing task. Tons and tons of bridging and track material, carefully positioned at all three corps maintenance areas in October-November, came in handy. Simultaneously, 900 km of border roads had been constructed or improved by the Border Roads Organisation and Army engineers to act as feeders to the Indian Army's thrust lines.

While talking about logistics, Lieutenant General Jacob, the Chief of Staff of Eastern Command during the 1971 war, revealed that bridging was one of the significant problems faced. Although we had worked out the quantum of bridging required based on the draft outline plan and sent out our requirements to the Army Headquarters in June, no physical material movement took place until mid-August. The bridging we got was nearly all of World War II vintage—Bailey Pontoon and FBE from the numerous depots spread throughout India. The modern, serviceable bridging equipment was kept in reserve for the western theatre, which remained unutilised. A little over half the folding boats were in position at the commencement of operations. Assault boats arrived late and were in position only a few days before the advent of hostilities. Most of the equipment needed significant repairs, and it was we who had to arrange for the repairs. However, the bridging equipment was repaired, and the dedicated efforts of the Chief Engineer and his staff saw to it that it was ready by the time we needed it.

The greatest difficulty was experienced in the movement of stores to the corps maintenance areas. Fortunately, the movement started in July, and we could complete it before the operations commenced. The corps dumps were established at Teliamura, Udaipur, and Dharamnagar. Around 30,000 tons of stores were moved to their locations in Tripura for IV Corps, 14,000 tons to Krishannagar for II Corps, 7,000 tons to Raigarh for XXXIII Corps, and 4,000 tons to Tura for the thrust to Dhaka.

Perhaps the greatest achievement of the 1971 war was the foresight in setting up a viable infrastructure and providing communications and logistical cover for the operations. Work had commenced before any operation order had been issued. It was a tremendous logistical achievement on the part of the administrative staff at command, corps, area, sub-area and the various divisional headquarters. When the hostilities did commence, our troops did not have to look back. Almost everything had been catered for. It was an outstanding achievement, and due credit should be given to all who made it possible, particularly the Brigadier General Staff, Adi Sethna, the Brigadier in charge of administration, Chajju Ram, and the Chief Engineer, Baba Bhide.

Important Tasks Carried Out by the Sappers in Various Zones

Though the Sappers carried out endless close support engineer tasks in the war to ensure quick movement of our formations to their respective objectives, certain high-profile engineer tasks that were carried out need to be mentioned. These tasks caught the world's attention and were even appreciated by the opposing engineers' commanders after the war.

I now touch upon the operations of II Corps, 101 Communication Zone Area and IV Corps in general, and XXXIII Corps in detail, as 235 Army Engineer Regiment was placed under the command of XXXIII Corps for operations in the sphere of the Eastern Command.

Operations of II Corps

Under Lieutenant General T.N. Raina, II Corps was responsible for the clearance of the southwestern sector, with the main objectives being Magura, Faridpur, Jessore, and Khulna.

9 Infantry Division was tasked to capture Jessore and advance towards Khulna. Jessore fell on 7 December, and the division's main axis was made trafficable within 24 hours, despite ten demolished gaps. The airfield at Jessore, littered with 50 craters, was repaired in a record time. Even BBC commented on the excellent performance of the Sappers.

The Battle of Khulna, and its capture, presented a formidable challenge. Khulna was captured on 17 December after the surrender of the Pakistani forces. 102 Engineer Regiment and 268 Engineer Regiment were deployed in this sector. The famous Jhinger-Gacha Bridge was constructed in record time and was later gifted to Bangladesh.

4 Mountain Division, protecting the northern front of 9 Infantry Division, advanced towards Faridpur. 58 and 63 Engineer Regiments were deployed here. The formation captured Jhenda, Magura, and Kushtia. In the east, towards Faridpur, the most spectacular was the construction of the bridge across the Madhumati River. It was a bridge of 1,385 ft length which was built in a matter of 36 hours!

The Madhumati Bridge became the longest bridge ever constructed by the Indian Army Engineers. It resulted from a joint effort of the 58 and 63 Engineer Regiments, using Bailey Bridge Equipment and Folding Boat Equipment. Advance resumed, and the troops reached the Padma River. However, by that time, surrender had taken place.

Operations of 101 Communication Zone Area

101 Communication Zone Area, under Major General Gurbux Singh Gill, was made responsible for the clearance of Jamalpur and Tangail, a prelude to the capture of Dhaka, while Mymensingh was to be bypassed. The force was launched from the north, and the thrust of the 95 Mountain Brigade was directed towards Jamalpur and Tangail. Engineer support, provided by the Chief Engineer of the North Eastern Zone, Brigadier N.L. Berry, involved crossing the Brahmputra at Jamalpur by river crafts. This operation, too, was carried out successfully by the Sappers.

When Bakshiganj was captured, Major General Gill wanted to visit this area by road. Brigadier Hardev Singh Kler, Commander 95 Infantry Brigade, advised him to come a little later, and that too by helicopter, once area domination was complete. However, Major General Gill insisted on going by road. Both officers started in a Jonga, driven by Brigadier Kler. They had gone a short distance when one of the front tyres of the Jonga went over a land mine. The Pakistan Army had laid these nuisance mines all over to create a hindrance and impose delays in advances by our Army. The officers were thrown out of their vehicle by the blast. While Brigadier Kler escaped any injury to himself, Major General Gill had a leg blown off. Brigadier Kler immediately took him to the nearby Medical Inspection (MI) Room of 13 GUARDS. Since his injury was severe, he was evacuated in a helicopter to the military hospital at Guwahati.

At Tangail, the para-drop of 2 PARA regiment and a platoon of 411 PARA Field Company (under Lieutenant Tejinder Singh) achieved outstanding results. The Para Sappers repaired the Tangail airfield within 24 hours, making it fit to receive Caribous and other light aircraft. It resulted in 101 Communication Zone Area reaching Dhaka by the morning of 16 December 1971 and, thus, becoming the first Indian troop to reach Dhaka.

Captain B.D. Chattopadhya of 235 Army Engineer Regiment was attached to 101 Communication Zone Area, Shillong, in June 1971 for carrying out very challenging special missions inside erstwhile East Pakistan. He was nominated as the sub-sector commander of the area near Chhatak town, comprising Shella, Patherghat, and Bholaganj. The main tasks entrusted to him were training the Mukti Bahini personnel, carrying out sabotage inside East Pakistan, and disrupting their power supply, road and water networks. By continuously creating a nuisance for the Pakistan Army, the latter were confined to their lines and bunkers, not obtaining a peaceful night's sleep for days and months together.

Furthermore, the aim was to win over the civilian population in the area through friendly behaviour and not allow the Pakistan Army to carry out patrolling and to stop them from looting the villagers for food, livestock, women and money. After carrying out these tasks most successfully, to the entire satisfaction of the formation, he returned to the regiment in December 1971. He joined his company, i.e., 176 Construction Company, which was still deployed in Bangladesh to restore communications.

Operations of IV Corps

IV Corps, under Lieutenant General Sagat Singh, operated in the eastern sector with 8, 23, and 57 Mountain Divisions. The main objectives of IV Corps were Maulvi Bazar, Chandipur, Akhaura, and Sylhet. 108 Engineer Regiment (commanded by Colonel A.L. Suri), with 8 Mountain Division, captured Maulvi Bazar to cut off Sylhet. For the capture of Sylhet, a heliborne operation with 14 MI-4 helicopters (the first-ever by the Indian Army) was conceived. Sappers of 484 Field Company (Lieutenant Gopal Krishan) were co-opted in support of 4/5 GR, which was nominated for this heliborne operation.

23 Mountain Division operated towards Chandipur, ably supported by 3 Engineer Regiment, and was further reinforced by 62 Engineer Regiment. Their main tasks were the construction of tracks and ferries between Comilla and Dhaka.

The division was unable to resume advance temporarily to Dhaka. At this juncture, the engineers performed a resolute feat in support of the division. 4 Engineer Regiment rushed downstream from Ashuganj, towards Narsinghdi, in five steamer launchers. They manoeuvred the crafts through the demolished bridge debris blocking the way, which took them over ten hours. Once on the Meghna, they were reinforced, and thus, the timely construction of infrastructure was inescapable for the conduct of operations in East Pakistan.

57 Mountain Division, supported by 15 Engineer Regiment, headed towards Akhaura. All planning revolved around ferrying operations on the Teesta, which facilitated the capture of Akhaura. Part of the division headed towards Meghna and Ashuganj. On arrival, the troops were confronted with a demolished rail bridge and strong opposition at Bhairab Bazar. Two battalions, with a platoon of Sappers, were heli-lifted and secured the bridge east of Narsinghdi.

Operations of XXXIII Corps

Under Lieutenant General M.L. Thapan, XXXIII Corps was responsible for the clearance of the northwestern sector, which included important places like Hilli, Rangpur, Dinajpur, and Bogra (for the Orbat, i.e., the order of battle of XXXIII Corps, refer Appendix 'D'). Operations by 20 Mountain Division were directed towards Hilli and that of 6 Mountain Division in the north, in the Thakurgaon area. Due to the terrain configuration and the number of engineer tasks envisaged, apart from integral divisional engineers, i.e., 51 Engineer Regiment of 6 Mountain Division, 13 Engineer Regiment of 20 Mountain Division, and 411 Para Field Company of 50 Independent Para Brigade, 471 Engineer Brigade, commanded by Colonel Mahinder Suri, was also placed under Command Headquarters XXXIII Corps. This engineer brigade had the following units under its command:

11 Engineer Regiment

52 Engineer Regiment

111 Engineer Regiment

235 Army Engineer Regiment

651 Engineer Plant Company

342 Workshop and Park Company

585 Engineer Park Bengdubi Bridge Company Normal

1133 ASC Battalion

972 Transport Company ASC (Tipper) less one platoon

Extensive engineer support was, therefore, planned. The normal procedure of allotting a field company to a brigade was brushed aside, and complete engineer regiments were allotted to each brigade. This allotment was essential since the terrain was the biggest challenge in the whole campaign. The entire area of operations was strategically crucial due to the implied threat from the Chinese on the northern border. Furthermore, the enemy positions were extraordinarily strong at Hilli, Dinajpur, and Bogra; the first two did not surrender till the final days of the war.

Notable in the 71 Mountain Brigade operations on the Thakurgaon-Kantanagar axis were the construction of a 600 ft bridge across River Atrai and a 1,340 ft Class 9 bridge near Khansama (Major D.S. Alagh, Field Company ex 111 Engineer Regiment).

20 Mountain Division, under XXXIII Corps, was made responsible for clearing Hilli as their initial objective, and it was commanded then by Major General Lachhman Singh Lehl, VrC. 202 Mountain Brigade, which was part of the 20 Mountain Division, was, in turn, assigned the task of capturing Hilli, a strategic town in East Pakistan. The significant tactical importance of Hilli was the waistline linking Hilli with Gaibanda on the Brahmaputra. This strip of territory provided the shortest approach to cutting all road and rail communications through the middle of this sector, thus isolating troops in the Rangpur area in the north from the rest of the Pakistani forces in the south. This waistline offered the most attractive but obvious approach for any attacker in this sector.

Hilli was a railway station right on the border, and a vital communication centre, which blocked all direct entries to this waistline. The area in and around Hilli was flat, abounded with paddy fields and dotted with villages, ponds, and clumps of trees, with occasional marshes and numerous rivulets. During the monsoons and till November, the whole countryside was covered with paddy, jute, sugarcane and other crops. However, most of the crops, except sugarcane, were harvested during December. During early December, most of the tracks were dry and fit for use by wheeled transport, even though with some difficulty as this required heavy maintenance for sustained traffic. The water table was generally very high, and while the upper crust of the ground after the winter harvest appeared firm, it could not withstand the movement of the medium tanks. 235 Army Engineer Regiment was placed under the command of 20 Mountain Division to provide close engineer support to 202 Mountain Brigade for the capture of Hilli.

Role of the 235 Army Engineer Regiment

The 235 Army Engineer Regiment played a very crucial, heroic, dominant and decisive role by providing effective close engineer support to 202 Mountain Brigade. As the operations progressed, some engineer support elements from the Regiment were grouped with the advancing columns of the 66 and 340 Mountain Brigades to ensure speedy progress of operations. After that, the Regiment restored road communications from Hilli to Gaibanda and Dinajpur to Dhaka. The capture of Hilli proved to be the toughest.

Before covering the details of the Battle of Hilli, and the various tasks carried out by the 235 Army Engineer Regiment, it would be worthwhile to highlight certain tasks carried out by the Regiment as pre-D-Day tasks. We were located at Misa, near Nowgong, Assam, and were part of the 471 Engineer Brigade, commanded by Colonel K.B. Seth. The other units were 58 Engineer Regiment, 268 Army Engineer Regiment, 397 Engineer

Construction Equipment Company, and 22 Engineer Equipment Workshop Company.

The regiment moved from Misa to Kolkata (erstwhile Calcutta), 24 Parganas, sometime in February 1971 to help in the smooth conduct of elections as the Naxalite problem was then at its peak. They had challenged the conduct of elections in the state. This operation in aid to civil authorities was code-named Operation Hot Spot, and for this, the regiment was placed under the command of the 20 Mountain Division and camped at Barrackpore.

We carried out flag marches in our respective areas of operations much before the actual date of voting. These flag marches aimed at restoring confidence in the general public so that they could come out fearlessly and vote. It was more so because the Naxalites had warned that they would cut the finger of anyone who came out to vote! Therefore, these flag marches acted as confidence-building measures. The orders of Lieutenant General J.S. Aurora, GOC-in-C Eastern Command, to the formations were unequivocal—should one find anybody even raise his hand to throw a missile, shoot him and inform the police. It sent a clear message and shivers to all the trouble-shooters. The effect of deployment of the Army was so strong that only six miscreants were shot, including one by a jawan of the 235 Army Engineer Regiment.

After the smooth and peaceful conduct of the elections, which ended on 10 March 1971, barring a few stray incidents, the regiment was then employed to maintain essential services, as there was a threat of large-scale disruptions and strikes. The whole regiment was familiarised and trained in various installations like water supply, electric supply, thermal plants etc., and was geared up to take over these installations and run them effectively in case of a strike. However, nothing untoward happened, and the regiment returned to its permanent location at Misa, Assam, at the end of July 1971.

I had just been promoted to the rank of captain when, on 8 August 1971, move orders were received from the Indian Army for the regiment's move from Misa to Siliguri for its likely employment during the impending operations (Operation Cactus Lily). The NMB (no move before) given was 15 September 1971. Headquarters 471 Engineer Brigade, under a new commander, Colonel Mahinder Suri, moved to Siliguri earlier than us. 58 Engineer Regiment went under the command to 4 Mountain Division in II Corps, and 268 Engineer Regiment was under command to 9 Infantry Division, also in II Corps. 397 Engineer Equipment Construction Company went under the command of Chief Engineer, North East Zone, Shillong (Brigadier N.L. Berry).

Just a day before the unit's raising day, on 13 September 1971, orders were received from the Indian Army for the move of our regiment to Siliguri on 15/16 September 1971. Major O.P. Batra took the advance party of 46 Other Ranks (ORs) and moved by road on 16 September 1971 to reach Siliguri on 18 September 1971.

I was responsible for loading the regiment at Nowgong, the nearest railway station to Misa. To assist me in this task, Lieutenant Jacob Kuriyan joined me, who had just reported to the regiment on his first posting. The regiment, less 176 Construction Company, left Nowgong by a special train on 17 September 1971 and reached Siliguri on 19 September 1971. 176 Construction Company went by road on 20 September 1971 and reached Siliguri on 22 September 1971.

On arrival at Sevoke Road, Siliguri, many officers were sent for road reconnaissance and to collect information by interrogating the refugees and the Mukti Bahini personnel. It is worth noting that the area, even at that time of the year, was generally flooded, and in some places, even the roads were submerged.

At this time, two sets of the Krupman Bridge were received by XXXIII Corps. Ours was the only engineer regiment, out of all the corps engineer regiments, which had done training in Krupman Bridge in 1969 while at Chandimandir. Major O.P. Batra, Company Commander, 76 Field Company, demonstrated the Krupman Bridge's construction to all the engineer regiments under Headquarters 471 Engineer Brigade at the Bridging Training Site near Kamla Tea Estate. Colonel Mahinder Suri, Commander 471 Engineer Brigade, was so impressed with the demonstration that he wanted our regiment to organise a training camp for all the engineer regiments of the brigade to handle the Krupman Bridge. Accordingly, a training camp of three weeks was organised by 76 Field Company to impart intensive training in the handling of the Krupman Bridge.

Move of Bridging Equipment and Other Engineer Stores

235 Army Engineer Regiment was made responsible for transporting the complete bridging equipment and other engineer stores allotted to the division from 585 Engineer Park at Bengdubi, Siliguri, and 1133 ASC Battalion (Bridge Company) to Malda by broad gauge railway. This work involved a move of six train loads (approximately 300 wagon loads) for which 176 Construction Company was moved to 585 Engineer Park, Bengdubi, for loading into vehicles. 76 Field Company was moved to New Jalpaiguri Railway Station for loading these stores into special trains. On 17 October 1971, two platoons of 75 Field Company also moved to New Jalpaiguri Railway Station for loading of bridging stores. 75 Field Company, 76 Field Company, 176 Construction Company, and 415 Resources Company, commanded by Major J.M. Sachdev, SM, and assisted by me as the Second-in-Command and Captain V.P. Pathak, TEO (Technical Equipment Officer), carried out this task most meticulously, in a well-organised manner, in a matter of six days (20 October to 25 October 1971), with the complete cooperation of the Railways.

Soon after the first train left for Malda, I was ordered to move there by road to receive and organise a temporary store dump at the Malda Railway Station. Accordingly, a store dump was established at the platform to distribute these stores to all the units of 20 Mountain Division as per their allotment. Here, at the railway station, the regiment was provided with one pioneer company, in addition to the regiment's manpower to help the regiment handle these stores. Managing six trainloads of stores with innumerable items involved proper stacking, accounting (to the last pin), security, distribution to various units, and maintaining an update of the availability of each item was a tedious and herculean task. However, it was performed exceedingly well by the team of 415 Resources Company. At that time, there were no calculators. So, one of the reasons for the success was that Major Sachdev had a very sharp memory, was very good at calculations, and could rattle out figures about various items and their location at any given time.

The Battle of Hilli and Operations Thereafter

On 16 October 1971, Major S.R. Dharwadkar took the advance party to the concentration area at Ganga Rampur. Thereafter, the regiment moved to the concentration area, where it stayed for about three weeks. Here four officers—Captains V.K. Sahni, A.K. Kaul, K.K. Paul, and N.G. Nadgouda—joined the regiment on 2 November 1971 on posting from the College of Military Engineering (CME), Pune, as their degree course was suspended due to the impending operation, Operation Cactus Lily. On 7 November, 2nd Lieutenant H.S. Bajwa joined here on posting from CME after completing his Young Officer's (YO's) course. Before moving to the assembly area, to freshen up the knowledge, all ranks were given intensive training in the following:

- Mine laying and breaching
- Road maintenance and track construction
- Fieldcraft
- Bridging training

Some of the infantry units were also trained in the following activities:

- Arming and disarming of both Indian and Pakistani mines
- Laying and recording of mine fields
- Waterman ship training

From here, the regiment moved to the assembly area, the village Kamarpara, about 12 km short of Hilli, between the fourth week of October and the first week of November. However, 75 Field Com-pany and 176 Construction Company moved further ahead towards Hilli to occupy the brigade-defended sector.

At the cost of reiteration, but say it I must, the Battle of Hilli, in the north-western sector of erstwhile East Pakistan, was inarguably the most ferocious and savagely fought battle of the Indo-Pak War 1971. 235 Army Engineer Regiment had the proud privilege of being intimately involved in providing close engineer support to the 202 Mountain Brigade for capturing Hilli. The

Brigade Commander of 202 Mountain Brigade was Brigadier Farhad Bhatty, VSM, the erstwhile courageous commanding officer of 4 GRENADIERS of Assal Uttar fame. Lieutenant Colonel Rati Ram Malik, a very tough commanding officer, was commanding the 235 Army Engineer Regiment. He was an officer who would never accept defeat, whether on a playfield or battlefield.

The team of 235 at that time consisted of a set of very dedicated, selfless, fearless, and sincere officers, JCOs and other ranks (ORs) who would go all out to work for the glory of the regiment and the nation. The regiment's specific task was to evolve and execute the engineer support plan based on the formation's operational plans, and allocate resources accordingly. The riverine terrain and the large number of water obstacles, marshy and water-logged fields, demanded operations generally against the grain which required detailed planning. So, the planning team in the regimental headquarters was headed by a very mature officer, Major V.K. Anand, the Second-in-Command. He was ably assisted by Major J.M. Sachdev, SM, Captain Ravi Raichand (Intelligence cum Planning Officer), Captain T.L. Joseph, Adjutant, and me. Very sound engineer support plans were made to fit into the operational plans of the formations, always supporting and constantly revising the plans as the battle progressed.

The main, and immediate, objective of the offensive was to quickly wrest control of the communication centre at Bogra to cut off, and isolate, the Pakistani forces in the north from the rest of East Pakistan. The shortest, and the best way, to Bogra was through Hilli, which was partly in India and partly in Pakistan, with the Pakistani railway line running north-south. Assessing the area of responsibility and the enemy strength to be tackled, two additional brigades, i.e., 71 Mountain Brigade and 340 Mountain Brigade were allotted to 20 Mountain Division. 20 Mountain Division attack plan was as follows:

- 165 Mountain Brigade to hold the Balurghat Bulge, supported by13 Engineer Regiment.
- 202 Mountain Brigade, supported by 235 Army Engineer Regiment, to clear Hilli and advance along axis Hilli-Goraghat- Palasbari-Gaibanda.
- 66 Mountain Brigade, supported by 52 Engineer Regiment, to advance along axis Patiram-Samjia-Phulbari-Nawabganj-Pirganj and prepare for the possible divisional battle of Palasbari.
- 340 Mountain Brigade, supported by 111 Engineer Regiment, to advance along axis Gangarampur-Dinajpur and link up with 71 Independent Brigade. Thereafter, advance towards Saidpur-Rangpur-Palasbari.
- 71 Independent Brigade to advance along axis Islampur- Pachagarh- Thakurgaon- Dinajpur and link up with 340 Mountain Brigade and proceed towards Saidpur.

In Hilli, the enemy was holding defences which had been stocked, prepared, and strengthened over a long period. Built-up areas and ponds, surrounded by marshes and dense groves, had been converted into strong points to contain and checkmate thrusts aimed at a breakthrough or penetration. Every house had been fortified into a strong point. A large number of bunkers had two layers of overhead protection. In fact, some of the bunkers were so prepared that weapons from the top compartment could be fired in the lying position while a man could fire sitting or standing from the lower compartment.

These defences were so well prepared that field artillery shells had a negligible effect on them. Every pond had been prepared for all-round defence, and mounds had been burrowed through to make shell-proof boxes. Heavy machine guns were cleverly sited and located to the flanks to make a heavy toll on any assault force entering the defended villages.

The location and neutralisation of these strong points, so well concealed inside the villages, and others located well away from the flanks of the main defensive positions, posed a major problem during this battle. The enemy defences, sited for all-round defence, were based on a combination of built-up areas and ponds. Shell-proof brick shelters were constructed in large numbers and had been linked up with an extensive network of communication trenches. At Morapara, we counted 72 bunkers with overhead protection. This position had been linked with Chandipur and Basudeopur villages to facilitate reinforcements and adjustment within defences. The ponds in and around Morapara provided a serious obstacle to assaulting troops because of the depth of water. In conjunction with anti-tank and anti-personnel mines, these had been developed into an effective obstacle belt. Booby-traps and wire obstacles were also used extensively. Mutual support had been organised by siting heavy machine guns on the flanks, as well as dug-in tanks in the adjacent villages for an integrated mutual defence and to achieve depth in the defence. According to the Pakistani columnist Colonel Niazi, 'The fortifications here were a classic example of defence in the history of modern warfare.'

It was one of the best-prepared positions as Pakistanis had all along expected us to attack in this particular area. Morapara was about 500 m from our border, and Basudeopur was not more than 300 m from our BOP at Aptair. A Krishak aircraft was arranged to fly Lieutenant Colonel Shamsher Singh, commanding officer of 8 GUARDS, over the area of Hilli so that he could see his objective clearly. All the reconnaissance had been done from our side of the border and not from the direction of attack, which was planned from the north. Patrolling across the border was not permitted.

On the fateful night of 22/23 November 1971, 8 GUARDS moved in for the assault on the northern defences of Hilli (village Morapara), held by Pakistan's 4 Frontier Force (FF). 38 Medium Regiment, 100

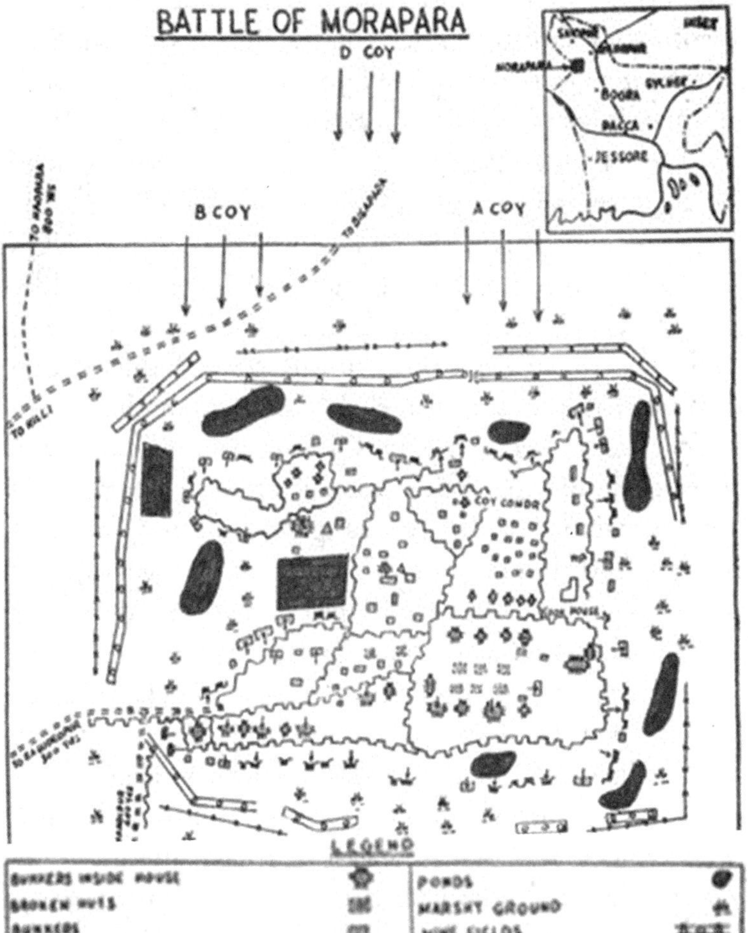

Mountain Regiment, and 37 Mountain Regiment had begun their bombardment in the afternoon. It felt as if an earthquake was striking. T-55 tanks and our 75 Field Company, commanded by Major N.S. Sohal moved in to support the attack. 'A' Platoon, under Captain K.K. Paul, was placed directly under the command of assaulting troops and did a commendable job in assisting the smooth move of forward troops to their objectives.

On 23 November 1971, there was a requirement of laying a minefield for which Second Lieutenant H.S. Bajwa, who had just come on posting after doing his YO's course, volunteered. One Section of 'C' Platoon, led by Bajwa, left at 1600 hours with 'A' Company of 16 RAJPUT to lay a minefield to the south of the existing Jamuna Bridge. The minefield was laid under heavy shelling and direct enemy small arms fire. However, without caring for their personal safety, Bajwa and his team continued with their assigned task and returned safely at 2005 hours, after laying 220 anti-personal and 60 anti-tank mines. It was Bajwa's first experience of handling live mines, and that too in actual war.

Incidentally, 4 Frontier Force was the battalion commanded by General (later Field Marshal) Sam Manekshaw, MC, before partition. The frontal attack on the Pakistani fortifications took a heavy toll on both sides. The brigade was able to break through after days of intense fighting, only on 10 December 1971, after we established a block in the enemy's rear. Thereafter enemy troops at Hilli withdrew towards Bogra.

Hilli turned out to be the only battle that the Indian Army fought to capture a Pakistani fortress in the entire campaign, and it proved very costly in terms of casualties and time. 8 GUARDS suffered heavy losses – 70 were killed, including four officers and two JCOs, including one other rank each from 38 Medium Regiment and 235 Army Engineer Regiment. A total of 130 were wounded, including six artillery officers and four JCOs, of which two were from artillery and one from other ranks from the 235 Army Engineer Regiment. The Battle of Morapara accounted for about 50 killed and almost 100 wounded.

In the Battle of Hilli and thereafter, 75 Field Company lost three other ranks (Sapper Trilok Singh, Sapper Theba Tamang and Sapper Bhaskar). Amongst the wounded were one officer (Captain J.K. Barla) and eight other ranks.

While visiting the military hospital, Major General Lachhman Singh Lehl, VrC, was told by one of the wounded soldiers, 'Sir, do check how our men were lying dead at Morapara and Hilli. All would be facing the enemy.' Lehl, in his book, *Indian Sword Strikes in East Pakistan,* says, 'How right he was; no wonder 8 GUARDS and attached troops fought so well.' For the Battle of Hilli, 8 GUARDS was awarded three MVCs (including one for the commanding officer, Lieutenant Colonel Shamsher Singh), two VrCs, one Sena Medal, three Mention-in-Dispatches, Theatre Honour East Pakistan and the Battle Honour Hilli. Our commanding officer, Lieutenant Colonel R.R. Malik, was awarded Mention-in-Dispatches.

It may not be widely known that the Pakistani officer holding Hilli, Akram (Shahid), was posthumously awarded the Nishan-e-Haider, the highest gallantry award in the Pakistani Army. It is the equivalent of our gallantry award, the Param Vir Chakra. The commanding officer of 4 FF, Lieutenant Colonel M. Mumtaz Malik, was awarded the Sitara-i-Jurat, the second-highest gallantry award in Pakistan. Even General Manekshaw wrote a letter to the Pakistani Army Chief commenting on the fight put up by his old battalion in Hilli.

As per Brigadier P.T. Ghogale, VSM, who was the Adjutant of 8 GUARDS during the war:

> One field platoon of the 235 Army Engineer Regiment commanded by Captain K.K. Paul got attached with us at Balurghat itself to provide close engineer support for the attack on Morapara (part of the Hilli complex) in the third week of November. Captain Paul found some apprehension in the minds of soldiers of 8 GUARDS, and he immediately laid a dummy minefield of density 1 with three lanes duly camouflaged. The soldiers were asked to go through this dummy minefield. The soldiers broke only a few pots which were depicting mines. After this test, the morale of troops went sky high as seen on their faces. For this innovative idea of Captain Paul, all ranks of 8 GUARDS will always be indebted to him. The apprehension and fear of crossing the minefield were gone with this demonstration. Captain Paul's platoon successfully carried out many crucial tasks to further our battalion's operational plans, and he deserved an award, in my opinion.

PATTERN OF OPERATIONS-WAIST LINE

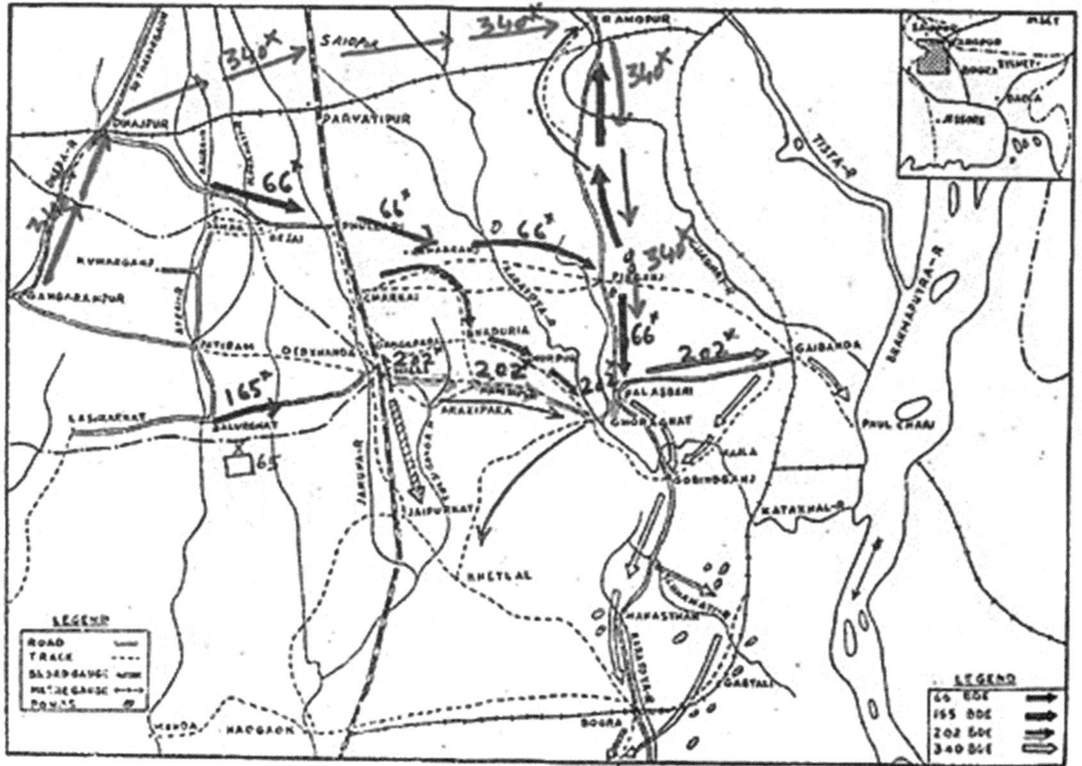

NOT TO SCALE

Team 235
Regimental Headquarters (RHQ)

Lieutenant Colonel
R.R. Malik, CO
Mention-in-Dispatches

Major V.K. Anand,
Second-in-Command
(later Lieutenant Colonel)

Major S. Dharwadkar,
Design & Planning Maj
(later Colonel)

Captain T.L. Joseph,
Adjutant
(later Major)

Captain Ravi K Raichand, Intelligence Officer
Commanded 234 Assault Engineer Regiment
(later Lieutenant General, retired as DG, Rashtriya Rifles,
awarded the AVSM for his meritorious services)

Subedar Major Jaya Nand
(later Honorary Captain)

Subedar Major Jaya Nand was very energetic, always cheerful, and well versed in his duties as a Subedar Major (SM) of the regiment. An SM is the main link between the officers and jawans. He knows the feel of the men and their morale. One of the main duties of the SM is to keep a close watch on all happenings in the unit and keep the commanding officer (CO) regularly informed. Every morning he is expected to report to the CO on all the happenings in the unit. His briefings normally end up with the traditional phrase, '*Baaki sab theek thaak hai*, Sahib—The rest is all okay, Sahib.'

75 Field Company

Major N.S. Sohal,
Company Commander
(later Lieutenant Colonel)

Captain Subhash Verma,
Second-in-Command (later Major,
first Adjutant of the unit)

Captain K.K. Paul
(later Lieutenant Colonel)

Captain J.K. Barla
(later Lieutenant Colonel)

Second Lieutenant H.S. Bajwa
(later Lieutenant Colonel)

76 Field Company

Major O.P. Batra, Company Commander
(later Brigadier, commanded the 235 Engineer Regiment)

Captain A.K. Kaul
(Second-in-Command)

Captain N.K. Bajaj
(later Lieutenant Colonel)

Captain A.K. Sharma
(later Lieutenant Colonel)

Second Lieutenant V.L. Vohra
(later Lieutenant Colonel)

176 Construction Company

Major Madan Mohan,
Company Commander
(later Colonel, commanded
the 235 Engineer Regiment)

Captain V.K. Sawhney
(Second-in-Command)

Captain N.G. Nadgouda
(later Lieutenant Colonel)

Captain B.D. Chattopadhyay
(later Lieutenant Colonel)

Lieutenant Jacob Kuriyan
(later Colonel, commanded
the 235 Engineer Regiment)

415 Resources Company

Major J.M. Sachdev, SM
Company Commander
(later Colonel, commanded the
235 Engineer Regiment)

Captain V.P. Pathak,
TEO
(later Major)

Captain R.B. Singh, Second-in-Command
(later Brigadier, commanded the 67 Engineer
Bridge Regiment, PMP*)
*Pomtomo Mostovoy Park—a Russian bridge

Headquarter Company

Major Hukam Chand,
Company Commander
(later Colonel, commanded
the 235 Engineer Regiment)

Captain Karam Singh,
Quarter Master
(later Lieutenant Colonel))

Captain M. Sen,
Mechanical Transport Officer
(later Lieutenant Colonel)

Captain P.N. Bandopadhyay,
Regimental Medical Officer
(later Lieutenant Colonel)

Major Tasks Executed by the 235 Army Engineer Regiment

Since 202 Mountain Brigade met with stiff resistance at Hilli, and its advance was held up, certain changes in the operational plans were made. Accordingly, on 5 December 1971, 76 Field Company, commanded by Major O.P. Batra, and one platoon ex 75 Field Company, under Captain Subhash Verma, were pulled out of Hilli and diverted to 66 and 340 Mountain Brigades ex 20 Mountain Division to provide engineer support. These subunits provided mobility to the two brigades by constructing several Krupman and Bailey Bridges in record time and executing other engineer tasks like track maintenance and mine breaching. Unmindful of his safety, Captain Subhash Verma would always travel in the leading tank/vehicle and get down on encountering any obstacle on their axes of advance, thus taking suitable remedial action for resuming the advance. Our brave officers, Major S. Dharwadkar and Captain K.K. Paul followed the same drill on the other axes of advance. The significant tasks executed by the subunits of the regiment on different axes are given below.

Tasks Performed by 75 Field Company

As 202 Mountain Brigade progressed in clearing various features in the Hilli complex, the company carried out the construction of a command post bunker, maintenance of tracks, laying of mines, breaching mines from the captured complex, and clearance of road axis from Hilli to Gaibanda (a distance of 65 km). The company continued to provide close support to the 202 Mountain Brigade till the surrender took place. So intense was the involvement of 75 Field Company that they bore the brunt of all war casualties in the regiment.

Tasks Performed by 76 Field Company

76 Field Company, commanded by Major O.P. Batra, carried out the following tasks:

- Laying a Krupman Bridge over the Karatoya River at Kanchanduha—a 150 ft long bridge constructed on 9 December 1971. The bridge was completed in four-and-a-half hours, helping the formation's early build-up.
- Laying of a Bailey Bridge two miles east of Kanchaduha–an 80 ft double/single Bailey Bridge that took five hours for completion.

- Laying of a Bailey Bridge over the Karatoya River at Gobindganj. The retreating Pakistani forces blew the permanent bridge here on 12 December 1971. A replacement bridge, 110 ft, double/single, was constructed in six hours under enemy small-arms fire and intermittent shelling on the Rangpur-Bogra highway.
- Laying a Krupman Bridge over the Karatoya River at Ghora Ghat. A class 40, 90 ft long bridge was constructed on the night of 14/15 December 1971 in record time.
- Laying a Krupman Bridge over Ghagat Nadi near Rangpur. A class 40, 90 ft long bridge was constructed on 16 December 1971, just before the declaration of the ceasefire.

The company assisted the 13 Engineer Regiment in converting ten kilometres stretch of the Phulbari-Charkai railway line into a class 40 two-way road. This task involved the blasting and removal of approximately a kilometre of railway track at the Phulbari railway yard, blasting and removal of nearly half a kilometre of rail track at the Charkhai Railway Station, and the construction of five improvised bridges with the help of rail lines and other locally available material. It was a remarkable feat for the Indian Sappers. This track was used for the movement of medium guns to launch a successful attack on Bhaduria on the night of 5/6 December 1971.

Second Lieutenant, V.L. Vohra, reported in the regiment at Dinajpur soon after the surrender ceremony on 16 December 1971 and was posted to 76 Field Company. The first task given to him was the clearance of a minefield in Birpur, about 70 km north of Dinajpur. The Pakistan Army had expected the Indian Army to advance on this axis and, hence, mined it very heavily. It was Vohra's first experience of handling live mines. Vohra, and his team, carried out clearance of the mine field safely during the hours of darkness and completed their job by early morning. The second job given to him was to repatriate refugees back to Bangladesh at Teesta. Over 15 days, they were able to repatriate more than 10,000 refugees. The third job he did was a joint road reconnaissance of 52 major roads for their traffic ability, along with Second Lieutenant H.S. Bajwa. After completing their job, they were de-inducted to India on 12 March 1972.

Tasks Performed by 176 Construction Company.

176 Construction Company, commanded by Major Madan Mohan, carried out the following tasks:

- Construction of a 110 ft Bailey causeway at Hilli on the night of 22/23 November 1971, under intense enemy small-arms fire and intermittent shelling, to take T-55 tanks over a marshy channel short of the river Jamuna.

- When the enemy stalled the attack on the night of 23/24 November 1971 by 8 GUARDS and started shelling heavily in the area near the existing masonry bridge on the river Jamuna at Hilli, the need was felt for having another alternative bridge. A 300 ft long FBE bridge was constructed on 24 November 1971 A/N under intermittent enemy shelling and small-arms fire.
- Construction of a track with duckboards and Sommerfeld track material and clearance of mines near Naopara.
- De-launching of a composite bridge (400 ft span) south of Hilli, after the de-induction of armour.
- Launching a 90 ft double/single Bailey Bridge near the same site, after reducing the gap with the help of a dozer, for the induction of armour due to a change of plans.

The company was left behind after the de-induction of the Indian Army from Bangladesh, even after the surrender, to restore road communication between Dinajpur and Dhaka—a distance of 324 km. Major Madan Mohan, assisted by Captain Chattopadhyay and Lieutenant Kuriyan, constructed 17 Bailey Bridges of various sizes on the highways near the demolished bridge sites.

It also removed mines, IEDs, and booby traps planted along the roads and the berms and made all the ferry sites functional. Moreover, it trained the Mukti Bahini and civilians in launching and de-launching the Bailey Bridges.

After staying there for three months and doing a commendable job, 176 Construction Company returned to Siliguri in April 1972.

In addition, all the companies continued laying and breaching mines extensively along many axes in synchronisation, with changing formations, operational plans, and requirements. The regiment also had to maintain tracks on the various brigade axes due to the slushy and poor conditions of the tracks. The prefabricated track materials were not found adequate. Extensive use of bamboo ladder tracks was, thus, made. These were found very useful for taking a limited number of vehicular passes. 2–2.5 inches diameter bamboo was split into halves and cut into 2.5–3 feet pieces. These were tied together by means of binding wire or used signal cable with a 2–3 inches gap. Each roll was made 25 ft long. One roll weighed approximately 21-22 kg.

Tasks Performed by 415 Resources Company

The most responsible task of 415 Resources Company, commanded by Major J.M. Sachdev, SM, assisted by Captain V.P. Pathak and me, was handling all the engineer stores on behalf of 20 Mountain Division. This involved withdrawal, accounting and move-forward as per the planned priority of all the stores from 585 Engineer Park, Bengdubi, to the Malda rail head. Thereafter, an engineer store dump was established at the Malda Railway Station for the issue of stores to divisional units.

The company was also responsible for all earth-moving tasks to facilitate bridge launches and the maintenance of roads and tracks along with the field companies. It also ran a workshop to fabricate and improvise gadgets required in various tasks assigned to the regiment.

It was ensured that forward-deployed field companies did not have to look back, and all the stores required by them were delivered on site. Unmindful of personal safety, many a time, we volunteered to escort the vehicles carrying these stores and delivering them to the site. At that time, everyone was so excited that they wanted to see action and go as forward as possible.

Though the war ended on 16 December 1971, the war to sort out and account for every item procured from 585 Engineer Park, Bengdubi, continued for more than a year as huge quantities of various stores that had been committed on the ground had been left behind in Bangladesh. This involved survey boards and condemnation boards, which were to take stock of each item. This formality, too, was got done in a time-bound manner.

Tasks Performed by Headquarter Company

As they say, 'An army marches on its belly.' This part of the administration was looked after by Headquarter Company, commanded by Major Hukam Chand. In carrying out this task, he was assisted by Captain Karam Singh, QM (Quarter Master) and Captain Mantosh Sen, MTO (Mechanical Transport Officer). Before the war broke out, Captain Sen was attached to the headquarters of the 471 Engineer Brigade as a Liaison Officer. Due to a lack of good communication equipment (unlike the present), these liaison officers had a tough time delivering messages of the brigade HQ to various units and subunits inside East Pakistan. They were always on the move and generally sent off at night, always fully armed to face any eventuality en route. The RMO (Regiment Medical Officer), Captain P.N. Bandhopadhyay, provided the much-needed medical support throughout the campaign and saved many lives.

Factors Contributing to the Success of Operations

Specific factors that contributed to the success of this operation in a very short span of 14 days were:

At the political level, our late Prime Minister, Mrs Indira Gandhi, proved to be a very astute leader in leading the nation at this critical juncture. With her concerted efforts, she managed to keep all the big powers on her side so that the planned operation in Bangladesh could be executed without any hindrance from any quarter.

The timely and very accurate advice given by General Sam Manekshaw, the then Chief of Army Staff, to Smt Indira Gandhi regarding the timing of this operation was a significant factor. She, in turn, realised and appreciated the timing that General Manekshaw set. Had we gone earlier, we would have definitely got stuck in the marshy fields of Bangladesh and become sitting ducks for the enemy. There was so much work and preparation required for launching such a large force. (See Appendix

'B' for the interview given by General Sam Manekshaw to *Quarterdeck* in 1996.)

The meticulous and detailed planning by commanders and staff at all levels helped enormously, as did the excellent coordination between the three services, led by the then General S.H.F.J. Manekshaw as the Chairman Chief of the Staff Committee.

The creation of infrastructure – a road network – for the smooth induction of troops and stores into the forward areas and the sound, timely and effective logistic planning that was carried out by all the formation headquarters was a plus. Enough time was given for reconnaissance and rehearsals by all troops.

Mukti Bahini and the citizens of Bangladesh played a big role in helping us at every stage by giving us the correct picture of the enemy's strength, deployment pattern, equipment held by them, and their routine activity. They also provided us with detailed information about the terrain where we were going to operate. These highly-trained and motivated Mukti Bahini personnel made the life of the Pakistani Army miserable and confined them to their barracks/bunkers. The friendly support of the locals made our lives comfortable and secure as we did not have to bother about our local protection; these people acted as our eyes and ears and were one of the important factors in our winning the war.

Complete domination of the air space right from day one by the Indian Air Force helped us move freely during the daytime. The spectacular role played by the Indian

Navy to contain and immobilise the Pakistan Navy cannot be ignored.

Then there was the excellent role played by the Sappers to support such a huge operation. They worked day and night to provide quick mobility and passage to the assaulting troops.

Most important was the courage and tenacity displayed by our brave officers, the JCOs and ORs of the three services. It forced the Pakistan Army in the east to surrender in a matter of 14 days and, thus, cleared the way to establish the independent country of Bangladesh.

Main Achievements of the Regiment

75 Field Company provided dedicated and efficient close engineer support to 8 GUARDS and 202 Mountain Brigade for the capture of the strategic node of Hilli and the operations thereafter. Since 202 Mountain Brigade met stiff resistance at Hilli, and its advance was held up, certain changes in the operational plan were made. Accordingly, 76 Field Company, commanded by Major O.P. Batra, and one platoon ex 75 Field Company under Captain Subhash Verma were pulled out of Hilli and diverted, on 5 December 1971, to 66 and 340 Mountain Brigades ex 20 Mountain Division to provide close engineer support.

All road communications were made possible from Hilli-Ghoraghat-Palasbari-Gaibandah, and Rangpur-Saidpur-Dinajpur-Dhaka (a distance of 400 km approximately) by improving/maintaining roads and tracks, lifting all mines, booby traps, IEDs, construction of replacement bridges and making all the ferry sites functional. A total of 27 replacement bridges (seven by 76 Field Company and 20 by 176 Construction Company) were made. It was a record by any engineer regiment in the eastern sector.

Minimum casualties to our troops (fatal casualties – three ORs killed; non-fatal casualties – one officer and seven ORs wounded).

Others' View—Lieutenant Colonel C.P. Singh

The role of Army Engineers and, in particular, of the 235 Engineer Regiment, as observed by Captain (later Lieutenant Colonel) C.P. Singh:

> Yes, this regiment did a great job – it's a nostalgic memory. When my tank troop reached the Karatoya River, I was tasked to ferry the guns of the 100 Mountain Regiment on the deck of my amphibious tanks (PT-76) across the river while the bridge was being made. I ferried all the guns across. However, my tanks got bogged down on the far side in my last attempt. My squadron ('C' Squadron, 69 Armoured Regiment) could not stop as they were heading to capture Pirganj. With no recovery resources in the darkness, it was the 235 Engineer Regiment which towed my tanks backwards with the winch till they were afloat again, and I was able to catch up with my squadron. My sincere thanks to them. During this time, as a troop leader, I never crossed the tanks at one

point on the far side and did not take the capability of the equipment for granted. Also, I had a close association with Captain Verma, who travelled (56 km) on my tank while my regiment was outflanking Bogra at night to earn the battle honour of Bogra. Captain Verma helped clear mines on a subsidiary advance to the Gayabanda-Hilli axis too. It was all a mutual support to achieve glory.

At the surrender ceremony, at Bogra, on 18 December 1971, Colonel M. Suri and Lieutenant Colonel R.R. Malik met the commanding officer of the 13 Engineer Battalion (Pakistan Army). His appreciation of our Sappers sums up and speaks volumes of the good work done by them. He said:

> Sir, I simply admire the way your boys brought the division virtually on their shoulders over the most indifferent and unexpected approach. We could never imagine that such a large force could ever advance over a route which we had ruled out as impossible.

On the performance of the Sappers, Lieutenant General J.F.R. Jacob, in his book, *Surrender at Dacca,* had this to say:

> Perhaps the most important role played during my tenure was by the chief engineer. We had asked for 'Baba' Bhide. Fortunately, he arrived in time to organise the engineering effort for the upcoming operations against Pakistan. I made it clear to Bhide that his primary responsibility would be the bridging. This required detailed planning, obtaining the

equipment, repairing and making bridges serviceable, and most importantly, getting their correct and timely placement done. When hostilities did break out, the bridging, so essential to the movement, was placed where it was required and, almost in all cases, in time. Much of the credit for our success in the operations in East Pakistan should go to Baba Bhide and his Sappers, who had been deployed in erstwhile East Pakistan.

The superb performance of the Sappers must be commended. Despite the very late release of the mainly obsolete World War II vintage bridging, they were able to collect it from various depots, have it repaired, move it to the launching areas, and finally construct the bridges, thus enabling the troops to move and fight.

Some Interesting Incidents Worth Remembering

For the soldiers, there is a thin red line which divides the sane from the mad.

On 11 December 1971, to clear the Hilli complex completely, there was the requirement of clearing a minefield in the area of Basudebpur-Chandipur. For carrying out this task Captain J.K. Barla, a very brave officer and a silent performer (he was attached to the monitoring section of HQ XXXIII Corps but volunteered to join his company, i.e., 75 Field Company, and to be part of the action at Hilli on 2 December 1971), volunteered for this task. Unmindful of his personal safety, as some remnants of the enemy were still there in this area and were being cleared by 8 GUARDS, his 'C' Platoon and he operated behind them. Luckily, just before he left for Basudebpur, he found the mine-laying record form in the pocket of the captured company commander of 4 FF who was deployed at Hilli. This helped him remove all the mines and make the area safe (total enemy mines recovered were: 18 anti-tank and 218 anti-personal). Charlie Platoon of 75 Field Company, under Captain Barla, also cleared the 1,400 yds road of Hilli–Shermijgar. His men and he were constantly under small arms fire and shelling during this entire time. However, they carried on without caring for their personal safety. As they were reorganising after the completion of their job, a shell landed near them, hurting Captain Barla and four more jawans (Naik Satya Prakash Gandhi, Lance Naik Nachhattar Singh, Lance Naik Raghubir Singh, and Sapper Baldev Singh) and killing two jawans (Sapper Theba Tamang and Sapper Trilok Singh).

Once 76 Field Company was moving with their bridging column, they suddenly came under intense strafing by the Pakistan Air Force. As per the drill, all the men dispersed to take positions. In this process, one of the Army Supply Corps (ASC) drivers stepped on a mine, and one of his legs got blown off! Major O.P. Batra, the company commander, wanted to go and recover this jawan, but was stopped by Captain Amrish Sharma, who said, 'Sir, he is from my platoon and I will go and get him. You please don't go.' Without caring for his safety, Captain Amrish went inside the minefield and lifted this jawan on his shoulders and brought him on the road. This incident shows the dedication, love and care towards their jawans by the officers.

At one of the bridge sites, where we were to launch a Bailey Bridge, our vehicle, which was carrying the launching gear, got stuck and could not reach the bridge site. Launching gear is essential because one cannot launch a bridge without it. But, to our surprise, we found a launching gear left by the enemy while retreating! The Pakistan Army also used the same Bailey Bridge equipment of World War II vintage.

Once Hilli stood cleared, I was taking my bridging column towards Gaibanda. Very near to Gaibanda, I found a very fast-moving advance guard of our Army coming from Rangpur and rushing towards Bogra. On reaching Gaibanda, the commander of this column asked me the timing of my arrival. When I told him that I had just arrived, he said that if I had come 15 minutes earlier, I could have captured Brigadier Tajammul Hussain Malik (who was the commander of 205 Brigade, which had been deployed at Hilli) and that he had begun retreating towards Bogra.

Once we reached Dinajpur, we learned about the famous Kantaji Temple where I went to pay my obeisance. There the *pandit ji* requested me to clear the *mandir* complex of any mine or booby-traps that the Pakistan Army personnel might have planted. I immediately deployed my team and made the area safe. Pandit ji was so happy that he presented me with an idol of Kantaji. This precious piece of art was, in turn, presented by me to the regiment on its Golden Jubilee on 14 September 2015.

When the Regiment was deployed for election duties, the supremo of CPM, Sh Jyoti Basu, came to witness the counting of votes at his Vidhan Sabha constituency Ashok Nagar in 24 Pargana. Here Captain Ravi Raichand and his men were deployed. Since Sh Jyoti Basu did not have a pass from the magistrate of that area, Captain Ravi Raichand politely told him, 'Sir, please get a pass by sending someone to the magistrate, and only then will I be able to allow you.' This was blown up in the press the next day—The Army stopped Jyoti Basu from witnessing the counting of votes or words to that effect. But all praised this rightful act, and it got a big *SHABASH* from his superiors.

Bravery is nothing more than overcoming fear. It is not an intrinsic quality. Some men are brave when confronted with physical danger but buckle under moral pressure. Others are made of strong moral fibre and refuse to give in, even when the situation appears to be hopeless. Some are courageous under a particular set of circumstances but not in others. There were a number of those who were not able to repeat their 1965 performance during 1971. Probably experience had taught an instinct for self-preservation. Quite rightly, field command is considered a domain of the young.

—Major General Hakeem Arshad

The Bengalis are very cultured people. A love of fine arts is their hallmark. Their music is so rhythmic, and the language so sweet, that a song can transcend all barriers of speech and convey its spirit even without understanding of the meaning of each word. As an agitated group, however, they are like a swarm of honeybees – when disturbed, they go on rampage, without distinguishing between the culprit and the innocent bystander, and once excited, they seem not to care even of their own safety.

Some Photographic Reminiscences

Surrender Ceremony at Dhaka

Lieutenant General A.A.K. Niazi, Commander of Army Eastern Command, Pakistan and Governor of East Pakistan receives Lieutenant General Jagjit Singh Aurora, GOC-in-C, Eastern Command of the Indian Army and Bangladesh Forces

The Instrument of Surrender document being produced for signatures

Lieutenant General A.A.K. Niazi, Commander of Army Eastern Command, Pakistan and Governor of East Pakistan signing the Instrument of Surrender document under the directions of Lieutenant General Jagjit Singh Aurora, GOC-in-C, Eastern Command of the Indian Army and Bangladesh Forces

INSTRUMENT OF SURRENDER

The PAKISTAN Eastern Command agree to surrender all PAKISTAN Armed Forces in BANGLA DESH to Lieutenant-General JAGJIT SINGH AURORA, General Officer Commanding in Chief of the Indian and BANGLA DESH forces in the Eastern Theatre. This surrender includes all PAKISTAN land, air and naval forces as also all para-military forces and civil armed forces. These forces will lay down their arms and surrender at the places where they are currently located to the nearest regular troops under the command of Lieutenant-General JAGJIT SINGH AURORA.

The PAKISTAN Eastern Command shall come under the orders of Lieutenant-General JAGJIT SINGH AURORA as soon as this instrument has been signed. Disobedience of orders will be regarded as a breach of the surrender terms and will be dealt with in accordance with the accepted laws and usages of war. The decision of Lieutenant-General JAGJIT SINGH AURORA will be final, should any doubt arise as to the meaning or interpretation of the surrender terms.

Lieutenant-General JAGJIT SINGH AURORA gives a solemn assurance that personnel who surrender shall be treated with dignity and respect that soldiers are entitled to in accordance with the provisions of the GENEVA Convention and guarantees the safety and well-being of all PAKISTAN military and para-military forces who surrender. Protection will be provided to foreign nationals, ethnic minorities and personnel of WEST PAKISTAN origin by the forces under the command of Lieutenant-General JAGJIT SINGH AURORA.

(JAGJIT SINGH AURORA)
Lieutenant-General
General Officer Commanding in Chief
Indian and BANGLA DESH Forces in the
Eastern Theatre

16 December 1971.

(AMIR ABDULLAH KHAN NIAZI)
Lieutenant-General
Martial Law Administrator Zone B and
Commander Eastern Command (PAKISTAN)

16 December 1971.

Surrender Ceremony at Bogra

Major General Nazar Hussain Shah, GOC 16 Infantry Division (Pakistan), Brigadier Pannu, Commander 165 Mountain Brigade, and Brigadier Bakshi Joginder Singh, Commander 340 (I) Infantry Brigade

This picture was taken when the two commanders brought the Pakistan GOC from Natur for the surrender ceremony at Bogra

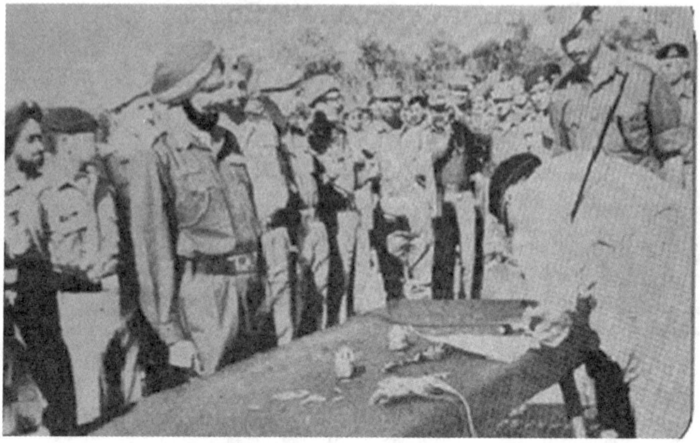

Major General Nazar Hussain Shah, GOC 16 Infantry Division, Pakistan Army, signs the Surrender Document

Major General Nazar Hussain Shah, GOC 16 Infantry Division (Pakistan), surrenders and offers his pistol and ammunition to Major General Lachhman Singh

Lieutenant Colonel Dutt is in the centre

Brigadier Bhatty with the artillery and engineer commanding officers at Dangapara

Captain R.B. Singh on the way to Dinajpur, Bangladesh

Captain R.B. Singh on way to Bogra, Bangladesh

Left: Captain R.B. Singh and Captain Karm Singh near a demolished RCC bridge, on road towards Bogra, Bangladesh
Right: With the replacement bridge made by the Regiment

Civil bus and locals going to Bogra over built-up causeway made by the Regiment

L to R (sitting): Major N.S. Sohal, Major Hukam Chand
Standing in the centre: Second Lieutenant H.S. Bajwa

Outside the officers' mess, Dinajpur, L to R: Captains A.K. Sharma, and T.L. Joseph, Major V.K. Anand, Captain M. Sen and Second Lieutenant V.L. Vohra

L to R (Sitting): Major V.K. Anand, Captain T.L. Joseph
L to R (Standing): Captain A.K. Sharma, Major S. Dharwadkar

L to R: Captain K.K. Paul, Major Madan Mohan, Captain Subhash Verma, and Captain Ravi Raichand

L to R: Major S. Dharwadkar and Captain Subhash Verma

L to R: Captain Subhash Verma and Captain K.K. Paul

Captain Subhash Verma relaxing after the surrender by Pakistan

L to R: Captain A.K. Kaul, Subedar Khanna, Captain Subhash Verma, Major N.S. Sohal and Captain K.K. Paul

Seeing off Captain J.K Barla (proceeding on posting) at the Siliguri railway station
L to R: Lieutenant A. Ghosh, Captains A.K. Sharma, Subhash Verma, J.K. Barla, R.B. Singh, M. Sen, and Subedar Govind Ram

Visitors too are welcomed

Epilogue

We lost the war without losing a battle. Even the enemy was surprised at the speed of our disintegration.
—Pakistan Army Major General Hakeem Arshad Quershi in his book, *The 1971 Indo-Pak War*

La vittoria trova cento padri,
e nessuno vuole riconoscere l' insuccesso
(Victory has a hundred fathers,
but defeat is an orphan)
— Count Galeazzo Ciano (1903-1944)

Finally, after carrying out innumerable Sappers and infantry tasks to the entire satisfaction of the formations and the units we supported (be it the occupation of a defended area, mine laying, mine breaching, neutralising booby-traps and IED's, constructing bunkers and command posts, constructing and dismantling bridges, water supply, constructing and maintaining roads and tracks, demolitions, repair of runways and any other tasks which required much improvisation), the Regiment got de-inducted in January 1972. It moved to the location vacated by 342 Engineer Workshop and Park Company and Transit Camp, Sevoke Road, Siliguri.

Since our Regiment was occupying a defended locality alongside the infantry in war for the first time, certain lessons that we learnt were that we must:

- Coordinate our defences with the neighboring locality.
- Ensure dedicated mortar and artillery fire power for our locality.
- Ensure reliable communication with higher headquarters and within the subunits.
- Have available adequate medical cover.
- Have constant liaison with the neighbouring units.
- Organise a daily briefing of all ranks for the various developments.
- Organise battle inoculation training during peace time.

When we left Misa for Operation Cactus Lily, all the off-road equipment and other equipment held by us as an Army Engineer Regiment and not required now (like stone crushers, sheet foot rollers, road rollers, etc.) for the pending operation and all other non-essential stores lying in the Rear at Misa were to be brought to Siliguri. Since I had the experience of loading the train when we moved to Siliguri and earlier also when we moved to Kolkata, I was detailed to wind up the rear and bring it to Siliguri in a special train. On landing at Misa, I discovered that the equipment we left in the rear had been lying off-road for very long and had to be lifted and brought to the railway station at Nowgong. Luckily, I could get a crane repaired, which helped me move everything to the railway station. When I brought the special train to Siliguri, our Commanding Officer, Lieutenant Colonel R.R. Malik, was so impressed that he asked me to brief all the youngsters on how to organise the loading and movement of the special train and demonstrate which all wagons were used for what purpose.

Many may not know that our Regiment motto

Sada Aage Sab Se Aage

was coined by me in 1979 when I was in Headquarters 416 Engineer Brigade as the Intelligence Officer (IO) and the Regiment was at Roorkee.

Never in the recent past will you will come across a campaign planned so meticulously that in a matter of 14 days, a country covering an area of 1,48,460 sq km got liberated from the clutches of the ruthless Army of West Pakistan and bringing them on their knees with the surrender of 93,000 highly trained troops. This was the biggest ever surrender after World War II.

Brave Hearts Who Attained Martyrdom

Army# 1408485—Sapper Madan Kumar Bhasker of 75 Field Company on 27 November 1971 at Hilii

Army# 1437341—Sapper Theba Tamang of 75 Field Company on 11 December 1971 at Hilii

Army# 1447230—Sapper Trilok Singh of 75 Field Company on 11 December 1971 at Hilii

Brave Hearts Who Were Injured

Army# 1408129—Sapper Chandeshawar Singh
of 75 Field Company on 27 November 1971 at Hilii

Army# IC-23185—Captain J.K. Barla
of 75 Field Company on 11 December 1971 at Hilii

Army# 1422386—Naik Satya Prakash Gandhi
of 75 Field Company on 11 December 1971 at Hilii

Army# 1400695—Lance Naik Nachhatar Singh
of 75 Field Company on 11 December 1971 at Hilii

Army# 1429072—Lance Naik Raghubir Singh
of 75 Field Company on 11 December 1971 at Hilii

Army# 1445221—Sapper Baldev Singh
of 75 Field Company on 11 December 1971 at Hilii

Army# 1459059—Sapper Ishwar Singh
of 75 Field Company on 12 December 1971 at Chandipur

Army# 1452048—Lance Naik Diwan Singh
of 75 Field Company on 13 December 1971 at Ghoraghat

The Regimental Song

Mrs Anju Vohra, wife of Lieutenant Colonel V.L. Vohra, composed a beautiful and well-meaning regimental song that encompassed all the tasks carried out by the Sappers. Thereafter, she sang it so melodiously that it has now become our proud regimental song.

Ye hai 235, yeh hai 235
Ye hai 235, yeh hai 235
Engineer regiment, Engineer regiment,
yeh hai 235, yeh hai 235

Janam liya isne Roorkee mein
San tha 1965
Ise banaya mahan sabhi ne
Veer bahadur hain sab
Ghar ye hamara hai
Jaan se bhi pyara hai
Boli ye himmat walon ki
Yeh hai 235, yeh hai 235

Surang lagana pul banana
Yehi hai humne dikha
Garmi sardi mausam ka
kabhi na humne socha
Retile teele hon parvat barfeele hon (2)
Ya ho zamee maidaanon ki
Yeh hai 235, yeh hai 235

Dushman kabhi jo saamne aaye
Door bhaga denge hum
Desh ki shaan ko uncha rakhen
Kam na hone den hum
Vachan hamara hai, pran ye hamara hai (2)
Sada nibhayenge hum
Yeh hai 235, yeh hai 235

Hausle buland hain apne
Unche aadarsh hamare
Jhukna kabhi na seekha humne
Kabhi na himmat hare, Sada aage sabse aage (4)
Yahi toh apna nara hai
Yeh hai 235 (4)
Engineerr regiment (4)
Yeh hai 235, yeh hai 235

Appendix 'A'

The Awami League's Six Points
Extract from Awami League Manifesto

Pakistan shall be a Federation granting full autonomy on the basis of the six-point formula to each of the federating units:

Point No.1
The character of the government shall be federal and parliamentary, in which the election to the federal legislature and to the legislatures of the federating units shall be direct and on the basis of universal adult franchise. The representation in the federal legislature shall be on the basis of population.

Point No. 2
The federal government shall be responsible only for defence and foreign affairs and subject to the conditions provided in (3) below, currency.

Point No. 3
There shall be two separate currencies mutually or freely convertible in each wing for each region, or in the alternative, a single currency, subject to the establishment of a Federal Reserve System in which there will be regional Federal Reserve banks which shall devise

measures to prevent the transfer of resources and flight of capital from one region to another.

Point No. 4

Fiscal policy shall be the responsibility of the federating units. The federal government shall be provided with requisite revenue resources for meeting the requirements of defence and foreign affairs, which revenue resources would be automatically appropriable by the federal government in the manner provided and on the basis of the ratio to be determined by the procedure laid down in the Constitution. Such constitutional provisions would ensure that the federal government's revenue requirements are met consistently with the objective of ensuring control over the fiscal policy by the governments of the federating units.

Point No. 5

Constitutional provisions shall be made to enable separate accounts to be maintained of the foreign exchange earnings of each of the federating units under the control of the respective governments of the federating units. The foreign exchange requirement of the federal government shall be met by the governments of the federating units on the basis of a ratio to be determined in accordance with the procedure laid down in the Constitution. The regional governments shall have power under the Constitution to negotiate foreign trade and aid within the framework of the foreign policy of the country, which shall be the responsibility of the federal government.

Point No. 6.

The government of the federating units shall be empowered to maintain a militia or para-military force in order to contribute electively toward national security.

Source: The Government of Pakistan White Paper

Appendix 'B'

Interview given by Field Marshal Sam Manekshaw to Quarterdeck (1996)

During the time of the 1971 war, there were personalities in the room, such as Admiral Nanda and Admiral Dawson. Can you recall anything about them in the period leading up to the war, or during the war, which you still remember, or which strikes you as something interesting?

> I can tell you before the war started. I can't remember the date now – sometime in April or something like that. There was a cabinet meeting to which I was summoned. Smt Gandhi was terribly angry and terribly upset because refugees were pouring into West Bengal, into Assam, and into Tripura.
>
> 'Look at this – so many are coming in – there is a telegram from the Chief Minister of Assam, a telegram from... what are you doing about it?' She said to me.
>
> I said, 'Nothing. What has it got to do with me?'
>
> She said, 'Can't you do something? Why don't you do something?'
>
> 'What do you want me to do?'
>
> 'I want you to march in.'
>
> I said, 'That means war!' and she replied, 'I don't mind if it is war.'

So, I sat down and said, 'Have you read the Bible?'

Sardar Swaran Singh said, 'What has the Bible got to do with it?'

'In the first book, the first chapter, the first paragraph of the Bible, God said, "Let there be light and there was light" – so you feel that "Let there be war and there is war". Are you ready? I certainly am not ready.'

Then I said, 'I will tell you what is happening. It is now end of April. In a few days' time, 15-20 days' time, the monsoon will break, and in East Pakistan when it rains the rivers become like oceans. If you stand on one side you can't see the other. I would be confined to the roads. The Air Force would not be able to support me, and the Pakistanis would thrash me – that's one.

'Secondly, my armoured division is in the Babina area; another division, I can't remember which, is in the Secunderabad area. We are now harvesting. I will require every vehicle, every truck, all the road space, all the railway space to move my soldiers and you will not be able to move your crops.'

I then turned to Shri Fakruddin Ali Ahmed, the agriculture minister, and said, 'If there is a famine in India, they will blame you. I won't be there to take the blame.'

Then I turned around and said, 'My armoured division, which is supposed to be my strike force, has got 12 tanks which are operational out of the whole lot.'

Y.B. Chavan asked, 'Sam, why only 12?'

I said, 'Sir, because you are the finance minister. I have been asking, pleading for months. You said you have got no money, that's why.'

Then I said, 'Prime Minister, if in 1962, your father had asked me as the Army Chief and not General Thapar, and your father had said, "Throw the Chinese out", I would have turned around and told him, "Look, these are the problems". Now I am telling you what the problems are. If you still want me to go ahead, Prime Minster, I guarantee you 100 per cent defeat. Now, you give me your orders.'

After hearing me, Jagjeevan Ram said, 'Sam, *maan jao na*.'

I said, 'I have given my professional view, now the Government must take a decision.'

The Prime Minister didn't say anything. She was red in the face and said, '*Achccha, cabinet char baje milenge.*'

Everybody walked out. I being the junior most was the last to leave and I smiled at her.

'Chief, sit down.'

So, I said, 'Prime Minister, before you open your mouth, do you want me to send in my resignation on the grounds of mental health or physical?'

She said, 'Oh, sit down Sam. Everything you told me, is it true?'

'Yes. Look, it's my job to fight. It is my job to fight to win. Are you ready? I certainly am not ready. Have you internally got everything ready? Internationally have you got everything ready? I don't think so. I know what you want, but I must do it in my own time and I guarantee you 100 per cent success. But I want to make it quite clear – there must be one commander. I don't mind, I will work under the BSF, under CRPF, under anybody you like; but I will not have a Soviet telling me what to do and I must have one political master who will give me instructions. I don't want the refugee ministry, home ministry, defence ministry all telling me. Now, make up your mind.'

She said, 'All right Sam, nobody will interfere, you will be in command.'

'Thank you, I guarantee you accomplishment.'

So, there is a very thin line between becoming a Field Marshal and being dismissed! It could have happened! So, that is one incident I can tell you about and you can put it in your own words.

What about the other two Chiefs? When did they come in?

They were not in on the initial meeting, then I had to brief them, I had to tell them about it.

Source: Quarterdeck, Directorate of Ex-Servicemen's Affairs, Naval Headquarters, New Delhi, 1996

Appendix 'C'

The Indo-Soviet Treaty of Peace, Friendship and Co-operation, 9 August 1971

Desirous of expanding and consolidating the existing relations of sincere friendship between them,

Believing that the further development of friendship and cooperation meets the basic national interests of lasting peace in Asia and the world,

Determined to promote the consolidation of universal peace and security and to make steadfast effects for the relaxation of international tensions and the final eliminations of the remnants of colonialism,

Upholding their firm faith in the principles of peaceful co-existence and co-operation between States with different political and social systems,

Convinced that in the world today international problems can only be solved by co-operation and not by conflict,

Reaffirming their determination to abide by the purposes and principles of the United Nations Charter,

The Republic of India on the one side, and the Union of Soviet Socialist Republics on the other side,

Have decided to conclude the present Treaty, for which purposes the following Plenipotentiaries have been appointed:

On behalf of the Republic of India:

Sardar Swaran Singh,
Minister of External Affairs,

On behalf of the Union of Soviet Socialist Republics:

Mr A.A. Gromyko,
Minister of Foreign Affairs,

Who, having each presented their credentials, which are found to be in proper form and due order,

Have agreed as follows:

Article I

The High Contracting Parties solemnly declare that enduring peace and friendship shall prevail between the two countries and their peoples. Each party shall respect the independence, sovereignty and territorial integrity of the other party and refrain from interfering in the other's internal affairs.

The High Contracting Parties shall continue to develop and consolidate the relations of sincere friendship, good neighbourliness and comprehensive cooperation existing between them on the basis of the aforesaid principles as well as those of equality and mutual benefit.

Article II

Guided by the desire to contribute in every possible way, to ensure enduring peace and security of their people, the High Contracting Parties declare their determination to continue their efforts to preserve and to strengthen peace in Asia and throughout the world, to halt the arms race and to achieve general and complete disarmament, including both nuclear and conventional, under effective international control.

Article III

Guided by their loyalty to the lofty ideal of equality of all people and nations, irrespective of race or creed, the High Contracting Parties condemn colonialism and racialism in all forms and manifestations and reaffirm their determination to strive for their final and complete elithination.

The High Contracting Parties shall cooperate with other States to achieve these aims and to support the just aspirations of the peoples in their struggle against colonialism and racial domination.

Article IV

The Republic of India respects the peace-loving policy of the Union of Soviet Socialist Republics aimed at strengthening friendship and co-operation with all nations.

The Union of Soviet Socialist Republics respects India's policy of non-alignment and reaffirms that this policy constitutes an important factor in the maintenance of universal peace and international security and in the lessening of tensions in the world.

Article V

Deeply interested in ensuring universal peace and security, attaching great importance to their mutual co-operation in the international field for achieving these aims, the High Contracting Parties will maintain regular contacts with each other on major international problems affecting the interests of both the States by means of meetings, and exchanges of views between their leading statesmen, visits by social delegations and special envoys of the two Governments, and through diplomatic channels.

Article VI

Attaching great importance to economic, scientific and technological cooperation between them, the High Contracting Parties will continue to consolidate and expand mutually advantageous and comprehensive cooperation in these fields as well as expand trade, transport, and communications between them on the basis of the principles of equality, mutual benefit, and most-favoured nation treatment, subject to the existing agreements and the special arrangements with contiguous countries as specified in the Indo-Soviet trade agreement of December 26, 1970.

Article VII

The High Contracting Parties shall promote further development of ties and contacts between them in the fields of science, art, literature, education, public health, press, radio, television, cinema, tourism, and sports.

Article VIII

In accordance with the traditional friendship established between the two countries, each of the High Contracting Parties solemnly declares that it shall not enter into or participate in any military alliance directed against the other Party.

Each High Contracting Party undertakes to abstain from any aggression against the other Party and to prevent the use of its territory for the commission of any acts which might inflict military damage on the other High Contracting Party.

Article IX

Each High Contracting Party undertakes to abstain from providing any assistance to any third country that engages in armed conflict with the other Party. In the event of either being subjected to an attack or a threat thereof, the High Contracting Parties shall immediately enter into mutual consultations in order to remove such threat and to take appropriate effective measures to ensure peace and the security of their countries.

Article X

Each High Contracting Party solemnly declares that it shall not enter into any obligation, secret or public, with one or more States, which is incompatible with this Treaty. Each High Contracting Party further declares that no obligation be entered into, between itself and any other State or States, which might cause military damage to the other Party.

Article XI

This Treaty is concluded for the duration of twenty years and will be automatically extended for each successive period of five years unless either High Contracting Party declares its desire to terminate it by giving notice to the other High Contracting Party twelve months prior to the expiration of the Treaty. The Treaty will be subject to ratification and will come into force on the date of the exchange of Instruments of Ratification which will take place in Moscow within one month of the signing of this Treaty.

Article XII

Any difference of interpretation of any Article or Articles of this Treaty which may arise between the High Contracting Parties will be settled bilaterally by peaceful means in a spirit of mutual respect and understanding.

The said Plenipotentiaries have signed the present Treaty in Hindi, Russian and English, all text being equally authentic and have affixed thereto their seals.

Done in New Delhi on the Ninth day of August in the year One Thousand Nine Hundred and Seventy One.

On behalf of the Republic of India	On behalf of the Union of Soviet Socialist Republics
(Sd.–Sardar Swaran Singh)	(Sd.–A. A. Gromyko)
Minister of External Affairs	Minister of Foreign Affairs

Source: Suivivai, XTLI, October 1971, pp. 351-3

Appendix 'D'

ORBAT for Operations in East Pakistan, 1971

XXXIII Corps — Lt Gen M.L. Thapan

Armour
63 Cav less Sqn
69 Armd Regt
Artillery
HQ XXXIII Corps Arty Bde
Bty 46 AD Regt
Two Secs 4 Air Op Flt
15 Air Op Flt
Engineers
CE XXXIII Corps
HQ 471 Engr Bde
11 Engr Regt
52 Engr Regt
111 Engr Regt
235 Army Engr Regt
651 Engr Plant Coy
342 Engr Wksp and Pk Coy
585 Engr Park Bengdubi
Br Coy Normal 1133 ASC Bn
972 Tpt Coy ASC (Tipper) less one Pl

6 Mtn Div — Maj Gen P.C. Reddy

Infantry
9 Mtn Bde
5 Grenadiers
4 Rajput'
99 Mtn Bde
18 Sikh
11 Garh Rif
16 Kumaon
Artillery
6 Mtn Arty Bde

94 Mtn Regt (75 mm USA)
98 Mtn Regt (75 mm USA)
184 Lt Regt less one Bty (120 Brandt)
Engineers
51 Engr Regt

20 Mtn Div	Lt Gen Lachhman Singh
Infantry	
HQ 66 Mtn Bde	Brig G.S. Sharma
1 Guards	
6 Guards	
17 Kumaon	
HQ 165 Mtn Bde	Brig R.S. Pannu
20 Maratha LI	
16 Rajput	
6 Assam	
HQ 202 Mtn Bde	Brig F.P. Bhatty
8 Guards	
22 Maratha LI	
5 Garh Rif	
Artillery	
HQ 20 Mtn Arty Bde	
64 Mtn Regt (75/28 mm)	
95 Mtn Regt (75/24 mm)	
100 Mtn Regt (75/24 mm)	
33 Lt Regt (120 Brandt) 3	
8 Med Regt (5.5 in)	
Engineers	
13 Engr Regt	
340 Mtn Bde Gp	Brig Joginder Singh
Infantry	
4 Madras	
2/5 GR	
5/11 GR	
Artillery	
97 Mtn Regt (75/24 mm)	

71 Mtn Bde	Brig P.N. Kathpalia
Infantry	
7 Maratha LI	
12 Raj Rif	
21 Rajput	
50 Indep Para Bde	Brig M. Thomas
Infantry	
HQ 50 Indep Para Bde	
2 Para	
7 Para	
8 Para	
Artillery	
17 Para Fd Regt (75 mm USA)	
Engineers	
411 Para Fd Coy	

Appendix 'E'

Bibliography and References

War Diary—235 Army Engineer Regiment

Indian Sword Strikes in East Pakistan
by Major General Lachhman Singh, PVSM, VrC

Surrender at Dacca: Birth of a Nation
by Lieutenant General J.F.R. Jacob
(Manohar, 2001)

The 1971 Indo-Pak War
by Major General Hakeem Arshad Qureshi
(of the Pakistan Army)
(Oxford University Press, 2002)

God's Own: The Bengal Sappers
by Colonel R.B. Khanna
(Mrs Saroj Khanna, 2003)

1971: The Sappers War
by Colonel R.B. Khanna
(E-in-C, Army Headquarters, Delhi, 1995)

Appendix 'F'

Engineer-in-Chief: Lieutenant General B.N. Das

In the Lead: Eastern Command

Chief Engineer: Brigadier V.V. Bhide

2 CORPS

Deputy Chief Engineer: Colonel H.K. Kapoor

COMMANDING OFFICERS

Lieutenant Colonel S.S. Bhatia—63 Engineer Regiment

Lieutenant Colonel C.B. Ramesh—58 Engineer Regiment

Lieutenant Colonel M.S. Gosain—102 Engineer Regiment

Lieutenant Colonel K.C. Taneja—268 Army Engineer Regiment

Lieutenant Colonel R.S. Kalra—203 Army Engineer Regiment

33 CORPS

Chief Engineer: Brigadier L. Krishna Murti

Commander 471 Engineer Brigade: Colonel M. Suri

COMMANDING OFFICERS

Lieutenant Colonel M. Balakrishnan—13 Engineer Regiment

Lieutenant Colonel S.K. Jain—11 Engineer Regiment

Lieutenant Colonel J.S. Makkar—52 Engineer Regiment

Lieutenant Colonel K.K. Malhotra—51 Engineer Regiment

Lieutenant Colonel D.R. Mani—111 Engineer Regiment

Lieutenant Colonel R.R. Malik—235 Army Engineer Regiment

101 COMMUNICATIONS ZONE AREA

Chief Engineer North Eastern Zone: Brigadier N.L. Bery

COMMANDING OFFICERS

Lieutenant Colonel Virendra Ganesh—2 Engineer Regiment

Lieutenant Colonel B.C. Pathak—59 Engineer Regiment

Major A.K. Dewan—411 Para Field Company

4 CORPS

Chief Engineer: Brigadier Jagdev Singh

COMMANDING OFFICERS

Lieutenant Colonel A.L. Suri—108 Engineer Regiment

Lieutenant Colonel Joginder Singh, VSM—3 Engineer Regiment

Lieutenant Colonel O.P. Behl—15 Engineer Regiment

Lieutenant Colonel S.S. Khurana—62 Engineer Regiment

Lieutenant Colonel D.N. Dass—4 Engineer Regiment

Lieutenant Colonel S.K. Sarkar—234 Army Engineer Regiment

Victory Day Celebrations

Brave Hearts Visit Bangladesh

Every year, the Bangladesh Government invites around 30 Officers (who have participated in the Liberation War of Bangladesh in the Eastern Sector in 1971) with their spouses or dependants to witness their Victory Day celebrations in Dhaka. In return, the Indian Government invites Bangladesh Officers and their spouses/dependants to Kolkatta to see our Victory Day celebrations.

Brigadier and Mrs R.B. Singh visiting Bangladesh to witness Victory Day Celebrations on 16th December 2017. Seen here with Mrs Sheikh Hasina, Hon'ble Prime Minister of Bangladesh.

Brigadier and Mrs R.B. Singh witnessing the Victory Day parade at Dhaka.

Left: Brigadier R.B. Singh and Mrs R.B. Singh at the National Martyrs' Memorial in Savar, Bangladesh, for the wreath-laying ceremony.

Right: At the Banga Bandhu Sheikh Mujibur Rehman's residence.

Brigadier R.B. Singh with the Naval Chief (left) and Air Chief (right) of Bangladesh.

At the reception and dinner felicitation by the Bangladesh Minister of Liberation War Affairs, A.K.M. Mozammel Haq and other mukti jodhas.

Lieutenant General Ravi Raichand, AVSM, and his daughter, Renuka Raichand, visited Bangladesh to witness the Victory Day Celebrations on 16 December 2019. Seen here with the Bangladesh Lieutenant General Shafiqur Rahman, Chief of General Staff.

Bangladesh Naval Chief Admiral Asangze and Lieutenant General Ravi Raichand.

Bangladesh Air Chief, A.C.M. Masibuzzaman Serniabat and Lieutenant General Ravi Raichand.

Bangladesh Army Chief, General Aziz Ahmad, and Engineer-in-Chief, Major General Fazal Shayekhuzzaman, with Lieutenant General Ravi Raichand exchanging souvenirs.

Colonel Jacob and Mrs. Liza Kuriyan visited Bangladesh to witness Victory Day Celebrations on 16 December 2019.

Lieutenant Colonel M. Sen And Mrs. Major Anupama Sen visited Bangladesh to witness Victory Day Celebrations on 16 December 2021.

The author Brigadier R.B. Singh with Lieutenant General Ravi Raichand, Lieutenant Colonel R.R. Malik, Major General G.K. Sen and some other brave hearts of the 1971 War meeting after a gap of 32 years at the Bengal Engineer Group & Center, Roorkee, in November, 2003.